THE MANTLE I NEVER ASKED FOR:

CRUSHED, CALLED AND CHOSEN

ISBN-10: 978-1-7358756-5-1

LOC#: 2021900210

Publisher, Editor and Graphics:

Fiery Beacon Publishing House, LLC

(Fiery Beacon Consulting and Publishing Group)

Greensboro, N.C.

Printed in the United States of America.

THE MANTLE

I

NEVER

ASKED FOR

CRUSHED, CALLED AND CHOSEN

A Literary Work Compiled by
Brandi L. Rojas

Table of Contents

The Forward

By Brandi L. Rojas

The Foreword

By Brandi L. Rojas

"Nah. Bigger." — God

Seems a bit unfair, huh? We are born into this world not knowing the greatness we possess only to discover it as we live life. Even as you prepare to dive into this literary work, you may be sitting on the edge of saying YES to your call, but NO seems safe. Can I be your vote of assurance and say, that this is NOT the time to play it safe, but instead to go full in?

I often say that I have endured things in life that were never taught in formal "ministry training", and even to this day that has become even more true. Let me help you - with the mantle God has called you to, you will not know+ everything beforehand nor will you always feel that you have every necessary tool, but you do.   One my favorite movies, "Suckerpunch" says it this way:

"You have all the weapons you need. Now fight!"

As a mantle-holder, I will gladly admit that at times it felt heavy and fairly uncomfortable. There have been many days that I simply wanted to elect to let it go simply because it seemed easier only to realize that letting go meant letting go of what gave me life as well. As I prepared to write this foreword, I was reminded of a Facebook Note that I created in 2012, upon the news of my grandfather Nehemiah Troxler, the mantles he carried and how those mantles had somehow made their way to me.

"Full Circle"

By Pastor Brandi L. Rojas

"And we know that God causes everything to work together for the good of those who love God and are called according to his purpose for them."   -Romans 8:28

When we think of a circle, we think of it as an object or condition where there is no end, everything is continuously moving and in the midst of it change is not experienced. So often, we say that people do not like to change, yet it is in our nature to want to change and demand change when situations insist upon it.

When I was fourteen years old, I lost my father. I recall some of the events that took place that day - being in school and being called up to the office to be greeted by my brother. I remember him telling me what had happened to our father, and as much as he was hurting too, made it a priority to ensure my security, safety and comfort. I remember meeting my Grandfather on my Dad's side for the first time and just the overwhelming feeling of meeting someone new...someone who's bloodline I carried on the inside of me. That was the first and the last time that I saw my Grandfather, Nehemiah Troxler.

As years passed, my Grandfather became a distant memory, however the memory of my Father continued to plague me, causing me to feel his loss over and over again, especially on the anniversary of his death and of course Father's Day and on days where I was accomplishing something GREAT and just wished that he could be there to see it. I was around the age of twenty-one, when one day the Holy Spirit told me to "find my Grandfather." There was a tug of war, but it did not last long. In short, the day that I found him, he was on his death bed. His brother Gad said,

"BRANDI! Nathaniel's DAUGHTER?!"

And in that very next moment, my grandfather died.

I can honestly say that all of this, though heartbreaking and unfortunate, was all a part of God's perfect plan bring to where I am today. A year ago, as I was speaking with one of my Aunts (on my Father's side), she became so excited at the news of finding out that I was in ministry. She kept saying that she wanted to come visit because I was the FIRST female minister in their family line. In shock, I then began telling her about the next step, becoming an Elder....at which point she became even more excited and said, "you are the first female minister in our family, and now you will be the second Elder in our family line!!!" When I asked who the first Elder was, she smiled and replied, "your grandfather!" Humbled does not even begin to describe the feeling that came out of me at that moment.... a man I hardly knew and yet GOD saw fit to choose me to continue this legacy!

So, you see, life comes with all kinds of adversities, but God's Word holds true...ALL THINGS WORK TOGETHER! So, if you are sitting in the midst of a situation as you read this, not knowing what is going to happen next just know that what you are going through is there to PROPEL you in this next level in Him. If you are reading this and have not accepted Jesus Christ in your heart or maybe you have but have gotten off focus, God loves you so much, and despite what you have done, there is something He's given you, beyond grace and past mercy - it's called REDEMPTION! Every experience you have had up to this moment did not kill you for a reason! You are still here because it's all a part of God's process to bring you full circle.

So again I say....

"You have all the weapons you need. Now fight!"

The Mantle Is Who I Am

By Sharon Benissan

When I was given the title of this collaboration, it blew me away because it made me think about all of the things that I have experienced in my life. It was hard to begin this journey of discovery because there were so many things to unpack. When I think of a mantle, I cannot do so without reflecting on both the natural and the spiritual. Naturally, I always knew and felt I was different from my family, as I was growing up in a house with multiple families living there. I did not always understand why I always got caught doing the wrong thing, but those around me always seemed to get away with it.

One day my grandmother talked to me and shared a story about how she left home when she was thirteen years old; my grandmother raised me, so I always enjoyed hearing her stories. She told me that it was hard for her at home because of her stepfather so she ran away. She met some nice people, and they took care of her until she got married. The part that I loved about her story was fragrance of perseverance it carried.

My grandmother did not give up; even though she was just a child, there was a determination on the inside of her that caused her to keep going.

When I look back over the years and see all of the triumphs and victories I have had while facing insurmountable odds, it activated a faith that I did not know existed in me. As I grew up, I realized one of the mantles I had was doing what I had to do at a young age and being raised by my grandmother that had to do the same thing. I did not understand why I went through being raised by my grandmother instead of my mother but in that place, I had

11

everything I needed, and God's hand was beyond evident upon my life. My grandmother was successful in the path she took, being able to take care of herself at thirteen years old. She met and married a wonderful man and had sixteen children. She did not complain but did what she had to do for her family as a mother and wife.

I understand now, the different types of mantles you can have. When I think about how I took care of myself and my children at a young age against all odds and still made it, that is a mantle. My grandmother trained me right as a child and even when I did not want to have nothing else to do with church, the way I was raised stood up.

"Train up a child in the way he should go; and when he is old, he will not depart from it."

Proverbs 22:6

When you show a child the ways of God and how to be in relationship with Him, a seed is planted and all you have to do is sit back and watch it grow. I want to encourage all of you that are reading my story - know that there is nothing you cannot do with Christ being the center of everything you do. When I say the mantle is who I am, I mean it literally because though my grandmother passed, I remain as a testament, alive and well to tell the story.

The Silent Truth

When I was going through an extremely hard time in my life God kept my heart, mind, and spirit together. I remember when I desired to be married; I was not ready for marriage, but I thought I was. During that time, I was traveling a lot for ministry and met a lot of people that I wanted to connect with. The key word here is "I" because I felt like I could have whatever I wanted including a man. My ministry travels began with going to South Carolina with a Pastor that I was working with in ministry who had a mandate to set up services in that area. As we began to travel, there was a gentleman in the church that kept looking at me. I pretended not to see him, but he started asking questions about me. When service was over, I was told we were going out to eat to meet some of the other members in the church; I was a little skeptical but went anyway. While at the restaurant, the senior leader of that ministry started talking to me and asking questions that sounded quite personal. The strange part of this dinner was the fact that he was watching me the entire time at the table. When the dinner was over, he walked over to me and said, "It was a pleasure to meet you." I could feel something different coming off this man and his energy was speaking to me. We went back to the home that we stayed in for the weekend and as I was getting ready to lay down the Pastor told me I had a phone call. When I answered, to my surprise, it was the Pastor of the church calling to ask if I could ride with the other Pastor to his home for a meeting the next day. I told him that I would be there! The joy in his voice was unmistakable as he told me he could not wait to see me again. At that point, I knew something was up with him.

The next day we went shopping and looked around the city with him, and he walked beside me the entire time. When we arrived at his home, he asked to speak with me privately, but I would not so he asked the other Pastor to go with me. She acted as if nothing was going on until we arrived at his home. We went into the house and there was another man with him, and immediately it began to feel like one, big set up. It started feeling really strange when the gentleman started acting as if he was interested in the married Pastor. I was having a conversation with the other Apostle and asked if he set it up for us to be at his house, and he said,

"I just want to spend some time with you."

I did not make a big deal about it because as people we have to talk in order to find out if there is a connection. I

13

really enjoyed talking to him, so we exchanged numbers and he called me that night before I went to sleep.

The next day was the first day I was in service with him. This man was a preaching machine and immediately grabbed my attention. (How many of you know that does not mean a thing?) After the service, as I was driving back to North Carolina, he called me saying that he wanted to make sure I made it back safely, so we talked all the way home. During the week, he would call me before I went to work and before I went to bed like clockwork. I started thinking about this man a lot and could not wait for the weekend to see him again. My heart was beating so fast with just the thought of him because he was a very handsome man, anointed, smelled nice and was well known by the community because he taught accredited classes at the university.

When I was on my way back to South Carolina, he would check on me to see if I was okay. The more he would act concerned for me the more I was drawn to him. After dating, about a month later he proposed to me; the sad truth is I was having sex with this man and he was not my husband, but it did not matter to us that we were not married. I am not going to act like I am innocent because I could have walked away but I knew exactly what I was doing. I continued to be in a relationship with this man and he even had a special chair just for me in the church near him. One day as I was having a conversation with the Pastor that I was helping, she started telling me about the Apostle and said that the first day he saw me in the church he asked her who I was. She told him and he said,

"That's my wife."

I was surprised that she did not share this with me before. She said she thought he was just kidding until she saw us together. When we were dating (not courtship) we would engage in a lot of activities that unmarried Christians should not do, but we did not stop no matter the time of the day; I

14

am being transparent because I want my life to help the readers make better decisions than I did. I remember meeting him before and after service and we would just keep going as if our actions were normal. He told me that we were getting married anyway so it was fine. Although I knew better, he had me sucked into his web of sin and lust so deep that it felt right. He started giving me money and I just thought he was being a gentleman until he wanted me to be church treasurer and I could see he was giving me money from the church fund and not his pockets - I felt horrible! When I spoke to him about it, he downplayed it as if it was nothing and kept going.

The next week he wanted me to meet some of his friends, so we went to a house party. When I stepped in the house, I knew most of the people there because I had already met them. The strange thing was they were not with the person I met them with. There was a long hall in this house and couples were coming and going and I began to see people coupled up that should not be. I called the Apostle over to see what was going on, but he would not tell me the truth. I asked another man that was there, and he said that it was a party for swingers. I could not believe he put me in that kind of environment where everybody was sleeping with each other! I rushed over to him to confront him about the news I had just received confirmation of, but he played it off as if it meant absolutely nothing. I took his keys and drove myself back to my truck and headed back to North Carolina. I did not tell the Pastor I was helping that I was not coming back. I was so hurt that he would put me in that kind of environment so easily without telling me. Without a second thought, my decision was clear, I never wanted to see him again.

HERE WE GO AGAIN

I went back to work the following Monday. My phone was ringing so much that I had to get another extension because of the calls coming from him attempting to explain his actions. I did not want to hear anything he had to say because of how he had openly disrespected me. He would send me flowers, cards, and letters but none of that worked. One day, I was at my desk and he walked into my place of business. His attempts had gotten so bad that I had to call the sheriff's department on him! The worst part is he sent me a letter because he was going to be in my area and gave me the number of the hotel that he was going to be in after a service he was invited to. I did not understand why I went but something inside of me wanted to go.

I want to help all of you reading my story. When you have been called by God, anointed and equipped some things happen in your life that you do not understand. I do not want you to be hard on yourself because we all make mistakes. I want you to know that you can ask God to forgive you and keep living even if you need some therapy along the way.

Now back to my story - I was late getting to the service. After my arrival, I could not get into the service because he was watching me as I walked in and sat down. He pointed at me and wanted me to come to the front, but I did not go. When he got up to preach it was as if I had forgotten about all of the things we had gone through. I was looking at him and the spirit of lust fell all over me! I had already prepared for it in my mind - he wanted me to meet him after the service to have sex with him and I would be ready for it. The way I was thinking was not the way I should have because I was so caught up in this man (some of you may call it a "soul tie.") Later that evening, I responded to a booty call after a service with the Apostle who was the guest speaker.

As I think about that day, it made me see that I had yet another mantle I did not ask for. I could have fallen back into sin with him because my flesh was a mess and I wanted him as much as he wanted me but when you cannot pray for yourself and you do not know why you are doing what you are doing, the bible says in Romans 8:26-27,

"The Spirit helps us in our weakness. We do not know what we ought to pray for, but the Spirit himself intercedes for us through wordless groans and he who searches our hearts knows the mind of the Spirit, because the Spirit intercedes for God's people in accordance with the will of God.

This passage of scripture helped me a lot because I was actually trying to live right, and I prayed but there was something still inside of me that wanted to be with this man. When I could not pray for myself the Holy Spirit stepped in on my behalf. I actually went to the room but left because I felt so convicted. He came into the room and we talked a little, but I let him know I could not do this anymore. I thank God for giving me the strength to leave and not look back. I know that I can help someone else dealing with or someone who has dealt with the same thing and pray that this helps whoever that person is to begin their road to recovery.

I began to understand that you have to go through some hard things when a mantle is dropped on you and your life may take a complete turn but what is on the inside of you will always come forth. I want to encourage everyone to never give up on yourself regardless of where you come from or what you have been through. I want you to know you can always start over. The first step is to forgive yourself and know the trajectory of your life will never be the same. I pray that the following scriptures will help to strengthen you in this walk, as they all certainly strengthened mine.

He gives strength to the weary and increases the power of the weak. Even youths grow tired and weary, and young men stumble and fall; but those who hope in the Lord will renew their strength. They will soar on wings like eagles; they will run and not grow weary; they will walk and not be faint.

Isaiah 40:29-31

Blessed is the man who remains steadfast under trial, for when he has stood the test he will receive the crown of life, which God has promised to those who love him.

James 1:12

I can do all this through him who gives me strength.

Philippians 4:13

No discipline seems pleasant at the time, but painful. Later on, however, it produces a harvest of righteousness and peace for those who have been trained by it.

Hebrews 12:11

Whatever you do, work at it with all your heart, as working for the Lord, not for human masters, since you know that you will receive an inheritance from the Lord as a reward. It is the Lord Christ you are serving.

Colossians 3:23-24

The Traveling Word

By Ciltona Cawthorne

I am an encouragement griot, something that I did not want, nor envision myself doing. There were gifted storytellers on both sides of my family. My mother was an amazing storyteller and I loved listening to her talk. Her sister and my maternal grandmother from Pinehurst, North Carolina were also wonderful storytellers. As a young child I would pretend that I was asleep so I could hear their stories late at night. Their whispered voices would wrap me in comfort and lull me to sleep. My paternal grandmother from Antigua was a gifted poet. Each one of these women instilled in me that we were beautiful, strong, elegant black women from a rich culture that we should always be proud of. They all passed into their reward over twenty years ago and yet I can still recount from memory many of the stories they told, as can my daughter because I told them to her as a child.

The weight of being an encouragement griot can be very draining emotionally and spiritually. I have always loved to read and share the stories that I created, and I always wanted to encourage people to feel better, inspired and affirmed, but while I would encourage others, I only felt comfortable around my family and my few friends. I was shy and I did not like what I saw in the mirror and I did not like my voice. I suffered from low self-esteem and did not feel empowered. It would be decades before I embraced my gifts of storytelling and poetry and the responsibility of using my art to encourage, motivate and inspire. I had no idea the power that I possessed.

Traditional griots were historians, spokespersons, psalmists, diplomats, ambassadors, musicians, teachers, warriors, interpreters, masters of ceremonies, and advisors. Not every griot does all these things. In hindsight I have operated in this role since I was a pre-teen in junior high school. As a spoken word artist, I now use my poetry in written form and orally to educate, inspire and motivate.

Years ago, when I participated in a program at work to share cultural gifts, I presented two of my poems. At the end of the program a man I had never met pulled me into an extremely tight hug and clung to me as he whispered in my ear that the poem was just what he needed to hear. Days after that program, he would barely speak when we passed each other in the hall. I have had to learn that people will pull on me in their need, literally cling to me and then have no further connection to me later when they are healed or just feeling better. For a while I was upset by what I viewed as callous insensitive use of me for my gifts by people looking to feel better. I was hurt and saddened about being ignored and disregarded until the next time people, co-workers and so-called friends needed a feel better fix. I was resentful and tired of my shoulder being cried on, but then God and His Holy Spirit imparted to me that my gift is to be shared and used by people. People are supposed to pull on me for their healing and relief. That is part of my gift and ministry, and I should not expect emotional connection or lasting relationships from the people I help.

As my gift of being an encouragement griot develops, God has enlarged my territory and I have operated in the roles of an historian, spokesperson, teacher, warrior, nurturer and advisor. The Holy Spirit comforts me if I am feeling drained, and God strengthens, affirms and loves me. So, I no longer rely on people I minister to for emotional support and encouragement. I have learned to encourage myself. I understand that I have no control over how people love and respect me or the lack there of, but I can control how I receive and react to how people treat, mistreat or appreciate me or not. Strengthened by God and understanding who God says I am enables me to not internalize the negativity or lack of sensitivity of folks.

The traditional role of the male griot existed in a specific region of West Africa, but now American cultural institutions are utilizing the history of the tribal griot to teach and share black culture. The griot disciplines of oral tradition and community empowerment are being used by black women today to preserve our culture and strengthen our people. My daughter is a storyteller who uses the artform of film to share powerful messages and positive images of black people and people of color.
Senegalese director, producer and writer Djibril Diop Mambéty said,

"The word "griot," is the word for what I do and the role that the filmmaker has in society. The griot is a messenger of one's time, a visionary and the creator of the future."

I now understand and thank God for my gift to be an encouragement griot.

But earnestly desire and strive for the greater gifts [if acquiring them is going to be your goal]. And yet I will show you a still more excellent way [one of the choicest graces and the highest of them all: unselfish love].

1 CORINTHIANS 12:31 (AMP)

I Am Your Sister

My sister, my dear daughter speak power, life and abundance.

I am your sister

In life, in love, in joy, in and through trials, and in triumph

I am your sister indeed

I am your sister in the midnight hour

I believe in your turn around

I know that God will bring you better and greater

I know that you are greater than they saw

and you are more than enough and nothing like what they said

You are who God says you are

You are one of a kind, beautiful and unique

created by the ultimate Creator in His image

Grace, peace, joy, love, strength, affluence, and influence flow from you and to you

Wealth for generations is in your hands

Know these things, and rest assured that the Omnipotent God that created you for greatness is in you and goes before you

He will fight your battles and He has your back

My sister, my dear daughter

speak power, life and abundance for which you were created.

Wealth for generations is in your hands

Much love,

Ciltona-Your Encouragement Sister

The Designated Survivor

By Deborah Davis

I have always stated that I have experienced what third- world countries have been through. When I say that, many people do not understand. Even those who know me still cannot fathom all that I have gone through or even know what I have been through. My story is not a "woe is me" moment nor is it one that I seek sympathy for; it is a story of triumph and resilience. I do not look like what I have been through, but what I have been through should give you a new perspective of what people like me look like.

I came from a two-parent household, mother and father both contributing to society. My father was a postal clerk and my mother was a pastor. We moved around frequently due to my mother's ministerial assignments. I often wondered why I could not stay put and would have to move so much. My mother would tell me that her ministry assigned her to another city so we would have to end up moving frequently. I have lived in Greensboro, Elkin, Statesville (all in North Carolina) and even Florida. However, this is not the amusing tale of Gulliver's Travels.

My travels led to homelessness, depression, mental illness, homeless shelters, and truancy.

The "how it happened" remains to be a longer story than what happened; all I know is that my mother whom I did not know was suffering from mental illness, had a severe break. I was not sure what that was at the time, but I knew something was not right. The illness led to my father quitting his job and our house being in foreclosure. It started a domino effect in which life as I previously knew it – having anything I ever wanted quickly went to not having anything I needed.

At the start of my eleventh-grade year, I was not in school. I would look out the window every morning crying, knowing that my classmates were on the bus laughing and enjoying life. I on the other hand was at home not knowing what the next move was. I had a younger sister who barely understood what was going on since she was nine years younger than I. My mother was no longer working, and my father had resolved to do the same. The lights were out. The water was off. Heat was provided by kerosene heaters. We walked to Woodmere Park to fill up gallon jugs and plastic bags became our bathroom. I kept thinking,

"This can't be my life. There has got to be a better way."

My maternal grandparents attempted to help however my mother was solely against it. She blamed everything on my father for not following her in ministry as other couples that were displayed on television. She wanted to be the Jan and Paul Crouch, Bob and Brenda Timberlake, Creflo and Taffi Dollar, however all my dad wanted was to be able to feed his family with a good paying job since he was the only one out of nine siblings who had everything "together". As the days rolled by, I realized that three months had passed since school had started and neither I nor my sister were in school. I did not how I would even graduate without going to school. I became depressed and mad at the world as well as my parents. The God that we were serving left me to experience a mess and the bad thing was I had no control over it. I was a minor under eighteen who had never worked and was never allowed to work because my focus as a child was to get good grades. Unfortunately, I could not even complete those assignments because I was not in school.

Soon it was decided that we would leave North Carolina for good and relocate to Florida. My father decided to withdraw monies from his retirement fund so that we could start a new life.   In Florida, we lived in hotels using the discount books to receive the $20 and $30 rooms; eventually, a deal was made with the hotel for a discounted weekly rate. We established residency at a hotel room, a double room for four people. We were enrolled in school, so there was finally some normalcy happening as we began to make a new life in Kissimmee. I had friends and I was able to escape the reality of my homeless situation for at least eight hours a day.

Unfortunately, it was short lived because my parents were unable to find employment due to their own personal restrictions – a job in which both could work at the same time at the same place. After a while, the monies my father received from early retirement ran out and they were unable to pay for the room at the weekly rate. One manager felt sorry for us and allowed my parents to pay as much as they could. However, it was not enough to get us out of the hole. It was not long before the hotel padlocked the room due to nonpayment. It was that day that my mother decided to have us to stay in the lobby of the hotel in retaliation for locking us out of the hotel room. That night the police were called, and my parents were charged with defrauding an innkeeper. That was also the same night that I was handcuffed for the first time at age sixteen because I walked toward the police cars where they had my parents in handcuffs as they were put in separate cars. They resolved to place me in the back of another police car where I rode in the back seat handcuffed while my sister sat in the front in a seatbelt. Even though the policewoman was nice and removed the handcuffs from me when we got inside the police station, I felt violated, confused, angry, devastated and again hopeless.

Later that evening, I learned that I would be in the custody of the State. I really did not understand what that meant, so the policewoman explained that a social worker would come to get us. I pleaded with her and told her that I would go wherever they wanted us to go as long as my sister and I were placed together. She told me she could not promise anything, but she would tell the social worker my wishes. The social worker came in and talked with me for a few moments. It was all a blur and I do not even remember what she said - I just know I told her that my sister and I could not be separated. She told me that usually we would end up in different places, but she would try. About an hour later, my sister and I were placed in temporary placement of a home with a lady in Florida in the wee hours of the morning, around 3:00am. I was transported to school later that day almost as if nothing had ever happened. I told my closest friends, and they could not believe my story. They told me that they had my back but what could they really do? I was in this by myself however God was in the midst of my situation.

After a few days, we were returned to my parents, but they were ordered to go to court. The judge questioned their employment, finances, residential status and even sanity. It was court ordered that we enter a homeless shelter in Orlando for families and for my parents to gain employment. I had to move again. The homeless shelter in Orlando was nice. They had a full school cafeteria with breakfast and dinner. There was a computer lab and activities for families to engage in, however, we never participated in any activities other than breakfast and dinner. I was able to receive free lunch at my new school in Orlando because I was a resident of the homeless shelter. I liked the normalcy. We were assigned to one room where there were four bunk beds. I slept on the bottom bunk and my sister slept on the top sometimes. My parents tried to squeeze into a twin bed but later gave up that attempt. I had to make new friends, that was not that hard, but I realized a lot of what I was missing since I did not have a television and was cut off from the world. I did not care about it much because at least I could live through them. I could pretend that I knew about things by reciting what they said and look it up on the computer later. Life as I knew it was starting to come together, or so I thought.

After a survey of the parking lot, it was discovered that my parent's 1985 Toyota Camry had expired tags. There was a rule that all cars had to have current tags and current registration. Since we had been in Florida for longer than thirty days, we were considered residents. The head of the shelter stated that the car would need to be registered or else it would be towed. Unfortunately, my parents had not secured employment and my mother had no intentions of really becoming a resident of Florida. It was not long before we were back on the road traveling and running away from life.

My eleventh-grade year was never finished, and my schooling stopped in Orlando; school was out of session and real life was in session. In fact, my eleventh-grade year could be summed up in one class, "The Art of Survival". We slept at rest stops and took showers there. We found items to return at stores along with selling clothing that we had in order to get money for gas and food. If we were recognizable, then we would continue driving up and down the highway. At one point on our journey, I believe that my mother or father called my maternal grandmother to ask for money to be wired. A question was asked about our whereabouts – the kids. Once she learned that we were homeless and at a rest stop, she contacted the police. A state trooper found us and provided us with pizza. It was so much better than half a bologna sandwich. He warned us that the rest stop was just that a stop and not a permanent place. We started sleeping in Walmart parking lots or any place that was twenty-four hours. We even slept on the side of the road once which was extremely dangerous and scary. It was not long before another police officer found out that we were homeless and helped us get into a shelter, this time in South Carolina. It was a home for families with a thirty-day stay. When it was near the thirty day maximum, the manager asked what our plan was, but we did not have one. My mother was against returning to North Carolina because she felt betrayed by those who, as she said, "pushed her out of the city."

My father did not care where we were, he was just tired of driving. The only problem now was the car had a hole in the radiator. Duct tape could only carry the car so far before it heated up, melted and caused the car to stop. My father felt that there was no other solution but to call on his family to help us. He called his oldest sister to come to South Carolina and bring us back to North Carolina. When his sister came, my mother would not allow us to get into the car. He left and said he would come back for us. After some convincing with my mother over several phone calls, we eventually left and returned to North Carolina. Despite the move and the family rescue, homelessness remained. My mother was able to get in touch with a friend she had while pastoring in Thomasville and we were able to secure an apartment within the housing authority; the only problem was there was no furniture. The rent was paid but no furniture. I was told that people offered to provide us with furniture, but my mother turned them down. My maternal grandmother bought us groceries every two weeks and when we were low, I learned new culinary skills. I had ketchup soup, crabapple patties and learned how to ration out an eight-piece chicken meal for four people to last several days.

After we got settled, I was able to enroll in the twelfth grade and began calculating how I could graduate without having the credits of my eleventh-grade year; my sister was also enrolled in school. Normalcy was finally happening again, leaving me free to begin thinking about my future. What can I do? The high school had recruiters from several colleges as well as the military to visit us. The Navy was very visible around the school as well. I wanted to go to college, but I was not sure if I could even go and I knew my family did not have the money to send me there. I had taken the SAT and only scored a 1020 which was amazing because at the time, my parents were outside of the cafeteria waiting on me during my exam. I finally decided that I would toy with the idea and talk to a recruiter. I spoke with my dad and told him I could not stay in this environment because they were arguing every day and we were being neglected. He told me that he did not want me to go into the military, but he understood that I had to do what I had to do. He told me no matter what happens, I am to take care of my sister. I agreed and I knew I had to have a way out.

Somehow, I graduated from high school. Too many people in the town knew about my situation and somehow God made it happen that I was able to graduate on time. I remember in my drama class people talked about their hopes and dreams for the future. In that moment, I broke down and stated that I did not know - it was the first time I admitted to myself that my future was undecided. My teacher consoled me as well as friends. Despite my admission, I still was not prepared for the next transition.

Right when it began to feel like we were able to just "live," Social Services were called into our lives again. We were removed from our home and placed into foster care with a woman and her two kids. I cannot say it was an easy transition since I was allowed certain privileges and they were not but at least I had a bed to sleep and enough food for days. I was able to keep the clothes I had without any concern about whether they would be returned for cash and since it was summertime, school was not an issue. Despite being in a comfortable environment, and everything seeming to go well, I knew I had to do something for me.

I decided to call the recruiter for the Navy. I felt as if it was my only option but would provide a way for not only myself but for my sister. I entered the delayed entry program and had my start date of January 1998. I was going to be a sailor with the job as a radioman. Even though, I had my life set up, I felt like maybe I had another option. We were having scheduled visitations with our parents. It was during that time that I decided that I wanted to apply for college and come back to Greensboro where my grandparents lived, but in order to apply, I had to have my parents' signature. I decided that I would ask my mother who has a Master's degree if she would sign my papers for me to go to college. She looked at me, smiled and said "No." When I asked why she told me that she had applied at UNCG, they denied her years ago and that she could not understand why I would want to go to a school that did not accept her. Despite my disappointment, my dad said nothing in response to the denial. I was so confused by her unwillingness to further my education that I decided to end my visits with her and my dad. My sister continued to go for supervised visits until they stopped showing up for the visits. A social worker overheard the conversation and stated that since I was a ward of the court, DSS could possibly sign my paperwork. I was excited but did not expect much. She had me to go into the DSS office and explain what I wanted to do. The supervisor stated, "Sure. I'll sign it. I am always in favor of people wanting to go to college!"

In that moment, a total stranger sowed into my life and accepted that I could be more than my situation.

The application was due the very next day. I mailed off the application feeling as if it would be denied or not get there in time. A month later, I received a letter from UNCG accepting me as a freshman into college with the start date of August 1997. In that very same month, it was arranged for my grandmother to have physical custody of my sister and myself; legal custody of my sister happened months later. We both made it out!

As I reflect on the trials and tribulations of my life, I realize that God was with me every step of the way. I know people who have been in similar situations and the outcome has not been the same. I thank God for protecting me and keeping me and my sister safe. It is no wonder why I have a heart for the afflicted and have a listening ear for those who feel unheard. For I was just that person - unheard, unconsidered, undervalued, and unconcerned. Despite the "uns," I persevered through and made an undeniable and unbelievable comeback. You never know the depths of what it took to get a person where they are currently standing. Just know if they are standing, it means something to them. The answers to my problems were always around. Everything that happened to me happened for my good - it made me pay attention to the details where others may neglect them. It made me have a heart for the child that has been displaced several times and now there are behavioral issues. Please note I am no saint, but I strive every day to be better than my yesterday and I am determined to accomplish that and more.

I Never Asked to be A Fatherless Daughter

By Portia C. Frazier

Often one says, "God why me?" We know that we not supposed to question Him, but realistically we do. There were many days I sat back and said to myself,

"Why me God? Why do I have to endure this? I didn't ask for my life to be like this!"

Growing up I never realized the strength I would need to endure. As a young child there were things that I had to go through that could only be accomplished through God's strength. Everyone sits back and looks at the smile on your face not knowing the pain behind it.

I was a child with an absentee father and that was an unimaginable pain. Watching everyone else with their father, only to sit and wonder what could possibly be wrong with you was a though that constantly flooded my mind. One begins to question who they are and why they cannot have one? The questions echo,

"What did I do wrong?

"Why am I not good enough?"

A lot of questions begin to go through your head. I'm sure many people can relate to this.

The day comes when you think you have a chance to live your childhood dream because you meet him only to be let down in the worst possible way and the hurt becomes even worse. The questions you ask yourself becomes even more real. Going through feeling unwanted because you were born can begin to lead you down avenues that makes life worse. Depression becomes a cloak that you wear to hide the pain that it seems no one has the capacity to understand. As a young child, we are taught to be quiet and not share the things we have experienced that could be seen or viewed as an embarrassment. In a way, we are taught not to care or give any attention to the problem in a sense. I would go through so many things and could never understand why I had to be the strong person. Why am I the person always going above and beyond? Why am I the one who must endure situations where I had to be strong? I never had the opportunity to take time to sit in my weakness, and though there were times when I just wanted to sit back and just be weak, I could not.

So, I began to put on a fake smile and move on. When I think back to different situations, I really had to be strong and I could not understand why. I remember sitting in church one day and a Pastor said to me, "You are mean." At that point it hit different because I had heard this before from many people. They used to call me "mean" because I was very blunt; I walked around as if I only cared about myself, but no one ever took the time to really ask what was going on.

"Why do you act like this?", was never a question anyone asked me but truthfully, I felt as if I had to grow up a lot faster than most. As soon as I turned eighteen, I ran from what I thought was the cause of everything, when

34

really, I was walking into places that would force me to endure a lot more than what I bargained for. There were many days I sat back and said, "people always call me with their issues.... but no one ever calls to ask me am I alright?" Every time someone was in a situation, I was the one who came to the rescue.

It is hard to be the strong one because you never have an outlet so to speak. Everyone around you depends on you and leaves others thinking that never need help or a shoulder to cry on. There are plenty of times that I would just cry myself to sleep because I had no one to talk to or call to just vent or pray with. I always had a group of people, but it was people who always needed something from me but did not have the capacity to pour into me. Being strong can a blessing, though, because it is not something most can handle or endure, a badge of honor so to speak.

I always put other people's feelings and issues ahead of mine, but I soon learned that when you put others ahead of you constantly you began to drain yourself. I can remember times of contemplating suicide and even attempts because I was so tired of feeling like I had to take on everything alone. I felt is if no one would really care about me and that all they would miss is what I could do for them; it was a horrible head space to be in. There were several instances where I did not really realize just how strong I was until later in life. Although, as a child I experienced many different "daddy issues" I really did not see how it was affecting my adult life; for instance, I went from relationship to relationship in search of validation and love and got involved in situations that one should never be subject to.

It began when I was about ten years old, and moved to Brooklyn, New York to live with my father. This was all very new to me as I did not really know him or the life I was entering. This would be my first year of public school which was totally different in itself since I had previously been in Christian and Catholic private school. My grandfather worked hard for us to have the best education. This with the emotions of not really knowing him or understanding the major difference in lifestyle became my new dilemma. Moving to Brooklyn was a culture shock to say the least since I was raised in a Christian home where we constantly stayed in church and was sheltered in a sense. While in Brooklyn I felt as if I had to grow up very quickly. Being in the public-school system with people of different backgrounds exposed me to different things. Although, I now had my father in my life something was still missing. He was there physically but not present. There was still something that I was longing for.

After leaving there and moving to North Carolina, somehow, I thought things would get better. I was so hurt and angry that I began to act out as a teenager because I felt as if I had to always watch my stepsister and could not simply be a child. I began to fight my father physically whenever I felt he was doing something I felt was not right. (My actions were not right, but it did happen.) At the time I thought my response was the perfect answer and that maybe because of it, he would just leave.

There were times when he would disappear, and things out of our home would to. I did not know what was going on and wondered why my mother would have to go looking for him. "Why is our stuff gone," was the constant question. As I grew up, I guess he felt it was time to explain what was going on. I found out that he was doing hard drugs. This reveal only intensified my questions into something I never imagined having to ask,

"Why I must have the father on crack?

Why I can't have what my sister has?

While in the process, you do not really understand why something is or is not happening - all you know is someone that is supposed to be pivotal in your life, is not. At that point I began to see just how deep this really ran as his mother, father and sister rejected me as well and would do spiteful things to me to show me just how much they hatred they had. They would come get his other daughter, take her places, claim her, and leave me sitting there as if I was a stranger. His sister which is two years older than me would say things to me to hurt me emotionally. I would act hard as if I really did not care but deep down inside it hurt because I did not understand what I had done and felt as if me being born was the factor that caused so much hatred in their hearts.

I began to take that pain and hide it. I began getting into relationships with boys just to have someone to say they loved me. I allowed things from relationships that were not acceptable and stayed in the constant search for a love that I could never find. I began to allow people to treat me any kind of way just so they would stay in my life and would keep relationships I knew were not going anywhere but downhill. What I thought was love I knew, was not.

When I came of off life support in 2012, I made up in my mind I wanted to do better and be a better woman. Along with my confessions, I decided that I should try to be a better daughter and just maybe he would be a better father. While I was in the hospital, I was told that he needed a place to stay because he had nowhere to go, so I allowed him to come reside in my home. He was still the same person he presented from day one, however, while there, I did not require him to do anything financially. I never asked anything of him, but he never offered to help knowing I was out of work waiting on disability either. He later moved out, got his own place, and severed all ties with me.

Then, I started to experience things within my marriage. It took a hit, and I began to feel as though I would never have anyone and that no one would ever love me. After deciding the marriage was failing and not coming back, I went into to a phase of "turn up." I started talking to dudes and disregarded everyone's feelings including my own. I began to date guys with no feelings attached, meaning that I would date them but refuse to allow my heart to get involved. Eventually, my questions to God outweighed my response, so I decided to stop dating and trying to figure life out for myself. I was lost and had been down the road of trying to find myself so many times before and failed and in all honestly, I had scaled back some but had yet to cut everything and everyone off that kept me off course.

One day I had asked someone I thought was a friend for a ride to the store. I got in the car, but he decided to go a different route. He pulled off to a secluded area; I asked, him what he was doing because I only asked him to take me to the store. His response had me fearful for my own life as he slapped me and proceeded to rape me. After this, I went into a deep depression; as a result, my doctor decided to put me in counseling along with prescription medication. I never talked about this with anyone, but instead, walked around holding it in. After going into counseling and beginning to talk to someone, it began to somewhat open my eyes to things I needed to fix within myself. I started to pull myself together to recover from what had happened.

Throughout this time, I did not have contact with my father and did not speak with him until years later. When I talked to him this time, he was in the same situation as before and needed a place to stay. Although, I was going through a lot at the time and was not good emotionally or mentally at the time, I allowed him to come stay with me. So much was going on in that moment - I was drinking and smoking my pain away, was suffering depression because of my miscarriage and was being harassed and stalked by someone that I was with before. When the alcohol and weed could not fix the pain, I decided that I would just commit suicide and end it all. I tried it only to wake up in the hospital and get a call from him going off on me. He never asked how I was doing or even why things were the way they were. His ammo was simple - it was because he had gotten back on drugs and I was the one for him to curse out.

After getting out the hospital I was determined that this could not be the life that God had planned for me and I had to do something. This is the time where I truly began to focus on myself and began to learn things about myself that I never knew. You know sometimes you think you are over something because you do not care anymore, but you are not. I had been going through a situation where it was said that I did not deserve to be loved because I was on disability and that my husband should not be with me because I have health issues. In dealing with this, I realized it triggered something in me - I was not truly over the situation with my father and his family. As I focused on getting closer to God, I battled with the commandment to honor your mother and father and so much more. I was asking myself, "how do you do this with someone who will not do right by you?" I decided I would reach out one last time and see if there is any ounce of hope left. I tried, and he did not want to meet me halfway. I prayed about talking to him because I know how he is. I made up in my mind I could only control myself and if I do it in love and with respect, God will not count me out. I wrote him explaining the hurt and how I felt deep down inside. I apologized for not being right with fighting him and cursing him out. In response, he told me that this was not his battle to fight and blamed everyone else as to why he could not be a father.

In experiencing this I learned that a lot of times we take the easy way out of situations. It is easy to see the wrong in others but never one's self. Pointing the finger is always the easy thing but to look in the mirror at one's own self is the hard part. It was not until I began to look at the wrong I did, that I learned that I was taking the easy way out. it was not until now I can honestly say that God has delivered me from this. God showed me with this situation I was never fatherless because He was present the entire time.

The love of God is what I truly longed for.

It had been present, but it was not until I got delivered from myself that I was able to see it. This experience has also taught me that we must listen to hear and not listen to be right; when you listen to be right you will never hear what is truly being said. I learned that I was giving myself away to the wrong man the entire time and that the same effort I kept putting into every failed relationship including the one with my father, overshadowed my decision to turn to Jesus first. I now realize, I may be fatherless in the natural but spiritually I have a Father that love me unconditionally, in my right and my wrong.

"Purposed for the Platform"

By Pat Galloway

It is with much hope that this part of my story will bring salvation and restoration - to understand and know that like me, you can recover. My contribution to this collaboration is, "Purposed for the Platform". How many will agree that your path and process is yours alone? You were not created or built like anyone else!

Growing up I quickly learned my life was that of obscurity and poverty. My grandparents would be an influential bridge, one that would keep me from being a statistic. Growing up in a small rural town was difficult and was truly a place where everyone knew details of your everyday life. This indeed was a town and mindset I never embraced. My mother, Betty birthed my oldest brother and I out of wedlock and as a young girl, I could not comprehend the depth of what that meant. My grandparents and mother loved us immensely and though we were always protected a covered by them, we would still have to deal with the truth that my hometown would be the beginning of our intended demise.

It is important that I note that Eden and Leaksville exhibited Pharisee spirits and that it is not foreign to have geographical demons assigned to your life. I can vividly remember my mom, Rick and I walking down Anderson Street waving at neighbors; I was seven years old and my brother was five. My mom always stopped to speak and never met a stranger. Anyone that knows me can attest that I possess the DNA of my mom. We were walking to Byrd's Lo Mark because Mom never learned to drive. If we had no money for a Leaksville taxi, we walked. A lady who we had never met walked toward us. My mom was a few feet away looking at food. The lady looking at us in disgust expressed, "Ain't y'all Bug Hicks children?" Bug was my father's nickname. My brother and I shook our heads in a yes motion. The next words I still remember. Looking at my brother she said, "You will be nothing just like your alcoholic daddy." I remember the hurt I felt for my brother and the crushing of my heart. The lady whose face I cannot remember, looked at me and said, "You know y'all are bastards, right?" All I could feel that day was hurt, pain and dismemberment. My mom returned to us to find our unsettling expressions and immediately asked what was wrong. Still in shock, I said "Nothing mom," as we continued to walk down the grocery store aisle.

This was the first of many seeds the enemy planted to cause a spirit of worthlessness to be instilled in us. There was always embedded in me a root of uniqueness. Some of my own family members used to say, "You think you better than us," not realizing it was not personal. Deep down I knew I was better than my environment. Deep within I knew there was more to my life and that my mentality did not have the capacity to be contained to a box.

In my early elementary school years, I spent days sad and depressed. I was always bigger than other students and hated myself for it. When I was in the first grade there was a very cruel teacher named Mrs. Ivey. On time she taped my mouth shut and using masking tape, bound my wrists together. This very troubled teacher, then sat me in a cubby closet in the dark. The smell of old paint and musk filled my nostrils; afraid and traumatized, I urinated on my clothing. My little feet dangled as urine ran on the floor. I cried, wanting nothing more than my mom to come and rescue me. The call from the Principal came, expressing his support of this evil teacher. Needless to say, once my family came to pick me up, I had no desire to ever go back there again.

Most of my days were spent in sadness. The home environment was full of poverty and isolation. Growing up no one came to spend the night, there were very few visitors and we did not invite people over. There was a shame associated with others learning of our captivity and our closed doors held hurt, anger, abuse, and fear. The spirit of alcoholism was an evil monster, our boogie man. Angry at teachers I thought, "Why can't you save me?" Teachers lived in your neighborhood then. I realized then that people had the mindset of "what goes on in your house was and did stay in your house," and people kept silent unless it was gossip only to learn later in life that their own life was drowned in misery. I served and worked unselfishly and fervently never understanding how God could ever forsake me if He loved me so much. We were taught all of our lives that loving God made it all better. It was through the piercing feeling of being unwanted and unloved that the devil built the foundation of rejection.

Voices of the enemy came relentlessly, "You will never be good enough for God." The constant torment of fear, inferiority, people-pleasing and shame became the norm in my life. Perfectionism, pride, self-reliance and withdrawing from people was all I had come to know. The devil was devising a wicked plan to kill me. Beloved, freedom is necessary for effective ministry. Rejection has a root and can even be rooted in family origin! Many are in bondage today, and generational curses are producing the fruit of falsity in teaching and rearing. This spirit comes in authority forms as well. It comes to steal your value, worth and identity through vehicles of confusion and torment. Beloved trust me, YOU ARE ENOUGH. Walking in total unacceptance I was led astray by so many people.

I had forgotten details of some of my life experiences but in writing my story I prayed that God would send me vivid reminders, for in it my heart will be expressed to heal others! I will never forget a trip we took to visit family in another state. My cousins started talking about their sexual experiences, but I sat in silence as I was afraid to speak of my virginity. My cousins observed me not taking part in the discussion until finally, of my female cousins said, "Oh you a virgin?" I said, "yes," ashamed of my answer not realizing then this was a wonderful and sacred place. My cousin expressed, "We are having a party tonight. By the end of the night, you will have a man." Deep down I was fine with my virginity, yet listening to my cousin's opinion, I decided that virginity was stupid and useless. Later that night my cousins introduced me to Jukie, and boy did we talk it up and dance it out! My cousins later told me Jukie was taking me for a ride. As innocent as it sounded, I did not want to go, yet my desire to people

45

please took the place if my heart feelings and became one of the worst nights of my life. Jukie took me to his house and took full liberties with me. I can remember crying and asking God to please save me. After everything was said and done, this man drove me back to my cousin's house and I never saw him again. I remember crying and asking my cousins "why?" How could I be sold out by those I trusted and loved and why didn't I have the courage to say no? My cousins responded,

"Oh girl it gets better with time. You just hurt 'cause you was a little virgin."

I never told anyone because I believed it was my fault and as a result, I cried for what seemed to be months. I believed I was worthless, and no one wanted me. This is what happens to girls when we do not understand our worth; this place becomes a breeding ground for the spirit of assassination and a place where the enemy plants seeds of self-mutilation and anxiety.

Healing brings definition to who we are! Beloved the devil's initiative is to destroy the creation of who you were designed to be! Only when we understand our DNA is that of Christ can we recognize who we are! Only through my healing do I now realize that my family was dysfunctional. I forgave my cousins. I forgave the individual that raped me. Those persons operated from a junkyard mindset. A junkyard is a place where scrap is collected, waiting for recycling or to be discarded. God expressed in the healing process that we are allowing and have allowed dismantled, broken, torn down individuals dictate our life by desiring validation and acceptance from broken people.

Walk with the wise for a companion of fools suffer harm.

(Proverbs 13:20)

Go from the presence of a foolish man when they preceivist not in him the lips of knowledge.

(Proverbs 14:7)

The enemy stalled and hindered my progression however, he did not stop it! Your identity, your true identity allows you to be free. It took me many adult years to become free; the molestation, the rape, and impact of harmful words caused so much damage, nevertheless, to always be safe and wanted was my ultimate desire. Living in a very dysfunctional environment would push me into the arms of many men. Why you say? Because I wanted love and acceptance. I moved in with three other men over the course of time and found myself searching for qualities I did not possess only to discover that these men possessed no identity of their own.

I was a product of abandonment, low self-esteem, rejection, and multiple losses. Fear kept me from living a fulfilled life and I began to fall victim to the generational curses that would leave me a defeated foe. My prayer at five years old was, "God let me die so I can live in Heaven." Today I walk in victory understanding that fear is one of the first door openers, and a foothold to other demonic spirits. Men for me was an addiction and I pursued them not being fully aware how detrimental these soul ties were. Stalkers, verbal abusers, emotional and mental abusers seemed to be the result over and over again and soon my pursuit escalated to married men. Why would I settle for what seemed to be safety but whose only fruit was a lack of identity? I did all I could do to fill the holes in my soul by embracing any and all that would receive me, thinking that they would take the pain away. Beloved, no! Instead, it induced and perfected the pain. I became a victim of the devil's trap which later led me on a four-year process of purging a relationship in 1998 that was one of the deepest soul ties I had ever experienced. Losing this relationship brought with it a spirit of suicide and counts as the only time in my life I desired to kill myself.

The day I remember well. It was my birthday. We loved being together all of the time. I took a shower and dressed up for what I thought would be a date night. Walking out of the bathroom I hear a conversation.

"Hey baby, how are you?"

"Yeah, she's here in the shower." Fred expressed how he could not wait to get back in Dorothy's big bed. Thinking back now, I was very hurt and numb to be exact. The next thought came up as quickly as the conversation that pierced my heart:

"Pat you have nowhere to go."

I walked into the bedroom and cried until my eyes swelled. What a birthday gift right? Fred came to the bedroom and said, "I fell asleep on the sofa babe. I'll make it up to you." I never confronted him with the truth. Having a place to stay trumped having a broken heart. One day "Enough is Enough," showed up, Fred was confronted, and his lies led to my meltdown. I destroyed his entertainment system, pictures, and other personal items. Livid and completely out of my mind I picked up a butcher knife, all while promising to cut his throat. Thank God He intervened. Holy spirit came in a split second of reasoning. Dropping the knife, I expressed that I was leaving that night. I packed up all my belongings and drove to a minister's home. Crying all the way driving in the rain, the desire to drive into the eighteen-wheeler in front of me was overwhelming. Thank God I made it to my safe place! My friend prayed fervently for me as she anointed me with oil. The words were "God take this pain away. Allow her to sleep peacefully. I will carry this burden. She will be restored." For weeks to come she would minister to me. Being with her is where I would learn to war spiritually and be taught the purpose of worship and prayer. God would send many to groom me. This did not prevent the pain and issues of life as many came and still come to steal, kill, and destroy. The church hurt I suffered is too much to express; the lies, manipulation, and rejection are too much for this one chapter - that will be the next book. What I loved most in my life, betrayed me.

Growth in life did change my perception of love! Judging people and making love conditional allows the enemy to manipulate His people. I choose to see people as God does - through the blood. That same blood is what saved, redeemed, and restored me. God only sees through the blood. Every seemingly life loss and tragedy built me. Trusting Him sanctifies our thoughts and through that place, I have sustained and remained. There was so much change that had to take place, a metamorphosis if you will. I now realize that my tragedy was for someone's triumph! Today I rest in His creation. I am wonderfully and fearfully made and full of confidence and assurity! Validation comes from freedom in Him.

Being confident of this that he who begun a God work in you will carry it to completion until the day of Christ Jesus!

(Philippians 1:6)

God has called me to minister His word, an evangelistic mandate, an intercessor for leaders and pastors, a prophetic psalmist and modern-day Miriam. Beloved my value, your value is in the oil. What I endured and survived is for my value. The crushing is what exposes the value. In writing for this collaboration God reminded me that, "through you Pat I am anointing people with love and kindness." Your life always had purpose! Purpose and destiny are at the end. The crushing was in the progress of the journey - The Mantle I Did Not Ask For!

The Mantle

By Lin Johnson

The color of your eyes. The shape of your nose. Your smile. These are the things that everyone looks for and notices when a child is born, eagerly anticipating what was received and from who. It is easy for others to identify where certain attributes come from, though an infant has yet to identify themselves. As time passes, the commentary begins to include, "You act just like your mom/dad" or "You sound just like your mom/dad". I am sure we have all heard these things at some point in our lives, but have you ever stopped to examine exactly what that means? What did you inherit?

I am the challenging, audacious and often times, complex daughter of a woman that I did not always understand. Growing up, our perspectives, ideas, emotions and mentality seemed contrary at worst and incompatible at best. A mother-daughter relationship is one of the most important relationships any woman will have in her life. It is filled with power and perils and the journey of becoming who we are meant to be is a reflection of how we weather both. What makes the relationship with our mother so crucial to our development is the fact that they are not just the person who is in charge of nurturing us, keeping us safe and reassuring us we are loved - they are also our first role model as women. The perils implicit in this set-up are many and the power realized is invaluable. Added to those things, were the spiritual inheritance that I would receive.

I distinctly remember a time in my young life when I told my mom, "I didn't want to be anything like you, because you're weak." Yes, I am sure it sounded and felt, to her, just as harsh then as it feels writing it now. I was completely unaware of the weight of those words. I was intrinsically naïve to all that I needed from her, in her, and like her. What she carried was both kryptonite and courageous, inspiring and conflicting, drawing and repelling, and I did not want it. In my mind, she was much too saved! She was docile and my energy was far too demanding. Surely, I must have taken after my biological father, a man, though living, I had not known.

In order to understand the significance of a mantle, we must first understand what a mantle is. Though there are a variation of the meaning of "mantle" in the Bible, historically, the main idea is that of a covering such as a cloak or other article of clothing, as mentioned in Joshua 7:21 and Hebrews 1:12. The prophet Elijah "threw his cloak around [Elisha]" as a symbol of Elijah's ministry being passed on to Elisha. The prophet's mantle was an indication of his authority and responsibility as God's chosen spokesman (2 Kings 2:8). Elisha was not confused as to what Elijah was doing; the putting on of his mantle made his election clear. From the idea of something that "covers" in the natural, a mantle easily comes to represent spiritual covering also. A great example of a spiritual mantle which passed from one person to another is Elijah and Elisha.

Spiritually, some believe that it symbolizes the passing or transferring of anointing, calling or gift, as seen in 2 Kings

2:14; Elisha takes the mantle that had "fallen" from Elijah, and it is only after Elisha takes the fallen mantle, that he performs miraculous works (2 Kings 2:14, 21, 24). In the way that the Spirit descended upon Jesus at baptism (Matthew 3:16) and the voice of God declared him as the chosen servant, Elijah's mantle was more than the regular cloak that he wore. It represented his appointment as a Prophet of God. Before we go further, let's be clear. A mantle is not ours for the choosing, it is determined ahead of time by God. The desire God places in our hearts is just one indication, among other confirmations, of the calling that is ours.

Before Elijah was transitioned to heaven, he said,

"Ask what I shall do for you before I am taken from you." Elisha said, 'Please, let a double portion of your spirit be upon me.'"

(2 Kings 2:9)

It was Elijah's mantle which proved whether or not Elisha received his request. Elijah told him; "You have asked a hard thing. Nevertheless, if you see me when I am taken from you, it shall be so for you; but if not, it shall not be so." Elisha did see Elijah ascend into the Heavens. He then tore his own garment in two pieces and "took up the mantle of Elijah that fell from him." Thereafter, he also took up the work of his spiritual father and operated in his anointing.

The woman and preacher/teacher called by God that she is, I watched my mother journey through uncharted terrain and the winding roads of coming into the knowledge and practice of salvation. See, she was still new to the idea of church when she had me and my older siblings. When she studied the Bible, she had us study with her. When she began to fast and pray, we did the same (age and time appropriate). What she learned, we learned too. A divorced mother of four children, she was quiet, observant, loving and humble. Those things seemingly sound like amazing attributes, but it is some of those very things also caused discord in my young view.

All of my life, I have known, loved and watched my mother "church". Whether it be Sunday school teacher, auxiliary head, usher board president, choir member, choir president, preacher, secretary, announcement clerk, whatever the position, she had it, worked it and repeat! Every single time the doors of the church were opened, she was the first to arrive, whether by car, bus, taxi or walking and the last to leave, in the same manner with her four children in tow. I can recall my niece Jasmine, my Mom's first grandchild, at two or three years old, greeting her by saying, "Praise the Lord, Sister Wiggins!" That memory just made me laugh, in a bittersweet way. My mom loved church and we were her disciplined, obedient, happy and naïve children.

I am sure you have probably already anticipated the next sentence - I grew up in church. Yes, one of those. But as time would demand, I also grew up, developing my own perspective, opinions, feeling and thoughts. Like the rage of straight-line winds which can carry the destructive force of a tornado, I was changing. I watched the very thing that my mother loved, cause her tears and hurt, frustration and grief as well as challenged her to create an unending prayer life and an unyielding commitment. It angered me. I heard her cry at night, when she thought we were all asleep, asking God for direction and to forgive those that had trespassed against her. The fierce in my feistiness started as a young girl, watching her mother and innate role model, hurt over what she was teaching me to love; I would never, or so I thought. She moved with intention and assignment, no matter what went on around her and was never being or causing disruption. My spirit wanted her to STOP and REACT but she had the audacity to keep it movin'. I resolved that I was certainly NOT my mother and I would never do as she did. After growing up, I left the church. I told her, if that is what "this life" is, I do not want it.

I eventually returned to the church after being away for years, not because of what I saw others do but because of the things I had experienced with God on my own. At the time of my return, I was more appreciative of what had been passed down to me about my knowledge of God. I did not recognize then that He was calling me to assignment as well.

Years passed by and my mother's health began to decline. Among other diagnoses, I watched as my mom began her fight with breast cancer. She sat with the same quiet humility that I had seen before. She held her head up, with the grace I was familiar with her wearing. She was pained but never complained. Her body was weak but she pressed her way. As I carried her to surgery and all of the post-surgery appointments, I watched how, at every hospital visit, the doctors became more attached to her and even appeared to look forward to her presence. Every chemo treatment, the nurses seemed to gather around her, and clinched to every word that left her lips. Every radiation appointment, the staff came looking for her, just to say hello. She touched and prayed for each person that crossed her path. She left her life in God's hands, while working the assignment He had left in hers.

For a long season, Elisha was a servant to Elijah, supporting him in a menial capacity and learning at his feet (2 Kings 3:11). Joseph practiced servanthood for years—first he served his father, then Potiphar, then the prison warden—before he received the mantle and moved into mandate. David, who had been anointed king as a boy, sat and played his harp for King Saul, as he watched and learned. God positions you with people and leaders that He wants you to serve now. Serving with faithfulness and a teachable heart is a powerful means of being positioned to attain your God-ordained destiny. Jeremiah 29:11 tells us that God knows the plans that He has for us which means we do not know. We do not know His plan or how He will execute it for our lives. I have come to realize that the very things that was grievous to me was actually being packaged as a God gift. My maternal grandmother, who has gone from earthly labor to reward in Christ, declared while I was still a very young girl that I was "just like" my mom. No, I'm NOT, was my declaration of rebuttal. Fortunately for me, I am my mother's daughter.

As a divorced woman and mother of three children, ordained preacher, Sunday school teacher and lover of God, I have learned what it means to be tenacious, focused, driven and determined in my daily life by watching my mother navigate life's happenings as she depended on God. I learned that her tears were divinely ordained, as the weeping women are skillful in their call. I learned that my mother's humility was really submission to God's instruction and that her seemingly docile existence was her quieting the external noise of her flesh to hear the divine voice of God. Her silent prayers were ostensible battle cries. I have experienced hurt as deep as the soul can carry, and tears so heavy that my eyes became weary and swollen and pained in the very thing that I love. Along my journey, I have found myself searching for formidable tools and words of wisdom when navigating the assignment I was given. I search for my mother's voice. What I thought I did not want to be, is the very thing that I became, what has sustained me and what I long for,

To be an instrument of God.

Elisha's hunger and pursuit of Elijah was a sign of what God had placed in his heart. Elisha was appointed by God as Prophet and successor to Elijah—but God used Elijah to recognize, prepare and establish that appointment. Elisha needed to cooperate with the call of God on his life to receive the mantle that was his by God's appointing. God is seeing the big picture, from Heaven's perspective.

When Jesus came out of the waters of Jordan, Jordan represented transition. There is always a thin line or barrier that you must cross in order to get to your next or your new. The barrier between where you are now and where you are going is called transition. Have you ever seen a relay race?

There are four runners needed to make up a team in a relay race and a baton is passed to mark a change in runners. Each runner knows the responsibility of their position and though relay races have various lengths, they all take place with one goal in mind; to focus, weather the storm and reach the finish line.

Much like the baton, the passing of a mantle signifies a new carrier and another leg of the journey. Unlike the baton, spiritually, a mantle in the Bible is a sign of calling, election made clear, yet the goal is the same - to carry it well, weather the storm and reach the finish line. I am my mother's daughter.

Be encouraged. Whatever the mantle is that you have been called to, know that God saw you fit for the journey. Often times, it is not easy. Obstacles are inevitable, tears are warranted, and doubt keeps you humble and dependent upon the One who qualified you. It has nothing to do with us but everything to do with the need of the Kingdom. The mantle that I carry, I did not ask for but with diligence, vigor, and perseverance, I accept the baton of transition and move to mandate. Run your race. Walk with authority in your calling. Carry you mantle well.

A Mantle Worth Embracing

By Faith Makowa

Never forget that life is not about you - your existence is for God's purposes not your own. God created everyone with a purpose which align with their abilities. You learn how to work in agreement with God from a place of rest so that you can start living in your purpose. It is a battle that we live in this world that seeks to define us by its own standards and performances; if we accidentally engage in it, this could impact everything about us and we can easily focus on things that do not matter.

Every day we must ask ourselves, "How can we represent God to the world?" We all have a job description and responsibility, and we have to respond faithfully and wholeheartedly to the call of God. Life is a mystery - you may not understand why certain things happen in your life. To really understand everything, we have to move through each experience we encounter to become who we are meant to be, but your mindset can limit you to see your purpose. When we continue to look around at how other people operate, we can completely miss the God given mantle we already have. Since all of us are born with a purpose, we do not have to dig so hard to discover what it is but there are also times when God uses people to confirm it or you can develop a longing in your heart, or a deep passion about something when you follow God's ways that leads to the discovery of the greatness in you. That is how you know God is pointing you to something much more meaningful than just carnal or material identity or goals.

Before I unpack my own unique story of how I discovered that I had a mantle that I never asked for, I have discovered that knowledge is power and is necessary to help us make wise decisions in our journey of life. Hosea 4:6 speaks about lack of knowledge as the greatest advantage

59

for the devil to rob you of your blessing and led you into spiritual blindness or bondage. Many people face tough trials, times of trouble, terrible traumas, or find themselves placed in a situation anchored to be a place of great discomfort which may leave them weary and can place them in a survival mode. In the process we often forget that that someone once walked in those same shoes for greatness. It is also difficulty to recognise God's voice in the midst of the storm especially when you are crippled by fear and doubt, hard to believe God's promises.

When I came to the Lord I was zealous with a deep passion to follow the ministry of Jesus Christ. I had a burning desire to do great and mighty things for His kingdom and I could feel God's ultimate source of power burning within me. I was ready to set the captives free and ready to wear the mantle of Christ without fully understanding the price and process. it is like finding a gold mine and knowing that it will be of no good to you unless you put time and energy into mining and maintaining it. I had to find the meaning of life when I accepted Jesus Christ as my Lord and Saviour but to know more about His greater love I had to maintain my relationship, seek God's face daily and mediate on His word. By doing this my relationship with God became very strong, heightening my level of understanding in the things of the God. I began to rediscover who I was and unlearn certain things that I had believed in so called" man-made Christian's lifestyle." Then, I recommitted myself to the true church of Christ which was led by the Holy Spirit.

Born with a justice mind-set and empathetic personality, I always try to put myself in the other person's shoes to see from their perspective. I knew how it was to be broken, and how difficult it could be when one's soul was ripped apart to the place where one cannot indulge in anything even the Lord's prayer, requiring the need for prophetic intercession from others.

I realized that I was mandated for such a call - to ignite motivate, bring awareness, transform, heal, praying and help to stir up the gifts in others.

I prayed for people with a humble heart and heaven would respond miraculously yet I was just a nobody. I knew that I was carrying His healing power, which was overwhelming to those around me; I even witnessed miracles occur when my shadow would pass by.

We must always remember that we do not buy or ask God for a mantle because He has placed a call upon every believer in Christ; we are sealed and identified as the hands and feet of Jesus. Every believer is mandated to share the gospel of Christ. God will take care of us every step of the way. In the book of Jeremiah, Chapter 1, God appointed Jeremiah to be a prophet of all nations - this also implies to you. God Himself has appointed you to fulfil a certain divine assignment for His kingdom which must be carried out and complete within your lifetime. Where you are at this very moment is exactly were God wants you to be. He prepares us in different ways and when the time is right, He will make a way for you. God will connect you with those who have been created to support, provide resources and everything you need for your assignment. I am grateful that my sister Debra always encouraged me with her favorite quote, and it really helped me during my trying moments when I wandered far from God. She says,

"The kingdom of God is not for the weak in spirit you will always encounter challenges which wants you to throw in the towels and give up but be extremely focused and become a woman on a mission because God uses anything to express Himself, it is important to learn, understand and embrace the reality of your mantle."

"Embrace the reality of your mantle." Then I thought maybe I should look up the meaning in my science notes to refreshing my mind. According to science, a Mantle is,

"The part of the earth between the core and the crust is the MANTLE. It is made up of magma and rock,

"a covering"

But what is a mantle in the bible? According to the Old Testament it is an idea of "covering" - typically a large loosely feathery garments made of animal skin and a garment worn by prophets as a sign of their calling from God. Which made me wonder, if I was a prophet, how did I get this mantle and who has casted it over me? Well as you all know, those questions are not supposed to be know in advance. I remained undefined because I did not want to confuse myself with titles as I was still discovering and learning about myself and knew that I had to be patient. My focus was shifted from the mantle to Fashion Designing. Time passed by, until one day I was busy sewing a colourful dress for a function where I was going to be a speaker. As I was working, a vision of a fire appeared, and a man was lifted up in a whirlwind. As this man was lifted up, his mantle fell to the ground and a young man picked it up. Immediately I remembered the most exciting powerful and attractive story of Elijah and Elisha in 2 Kings 2:11-13 Where Elijah was taken to heaven in a whirlwind and where garments played a role.

¹¹ As they continued along and talked, behold, a chariot of fire with horses of fire [appeared suddenly and] separated the two of them, and Elijah went up to heaven in a whirlwind. ¹² Elisha saw it and cried out, "My father, my father, the chariot of Israel and its horsemen!" And he no longer saw Elijah. Then he took hold of his own clothes and tore them into two pieces [in grief]. ¹³ He picked up the mantle of Elijah that fell off him, and went back and stood by the bank of the Jordan.

Curiously, I opened my bible and begin to rediscover the story of Elijah wrapping himself in his mantle, then he cast his mantle on Elisha who embraced Elijah's cloak, and began to perform miracles. As soon as I came to my senses, I realized that the Holy Spirit confirms God's Word to us for a better explanation and makes it easier for us to relate to. I knew God was redirecting my steps back to my assignment.

Truly we cannot have inner peace if we do not address issues of mantles. I had withdrawn from my real call when I felt inadequate and unqualified. As for me I never had a mentor who casted a cloak on me, so I never experienced the Elijah and Elisha handover, yet I was operating in the realm of fire, miracles, signs, wonders and prophesying without a cloak. Several times God used me to release His healing and anointing to His people; the Holy Spirit guided my hand when I encountered people, and some overcame the adversary with the tangible presence of God. For years, many unspoken questions remained in my mind, but I read John 14:26,

"But the Advocate, the Holy Spirit, whom the Father will send in my name, will teach you "ALL THINGS" and will remind you of everything I have said to you."

This scripture helped me to understand the twenty-first century hand over incident better!

I had to trust the Holy Spirit for all my spiritual needs, teaching, corrections and revelations. The vision I had explained it all; I stopped questioning and beating myself about my sphere. Instead, I developed biblical core values and was convicted of my own worldly desires which led me to repentance and asking God that He remove anything that seems good to the world but was not aligned with my divine purpose that He had designed for me. I wanted to live purposefully and maximize my effectiveness in my family, community and world at large. God was faithful and His respond was just on spot!

After the fire vision on a Tuesday morning, the following Sunday my Pastor called me after church service and told me that I had a mantle on me and I was supposed to spend time in prayer, and ask God for the specific ministry He wanted me to serve in. Since he had noticed that I was a multi-talented person, he said that there must be one specific mantle I have been anointed for because sometimes God allows us to operate in other mantles if a need arises and there is no one who can boldly fill that gap. He encouraged me to share in church every Sunday whatever the Lord was showing me and to do what God wanted me to do, lastly, he said,

"Faith your mantle cannot be subcontracted, you must take your position and make His presence known in this church and around you. If you remain silent God will use a donkey to speak rather be obedient."

Smiling at me he continued, "though the price of the mantle is high it's always been costly and it's a price you must be willing to pay." He stopped speaking for a moment and then continued, "don't be afraid of making mistakes or fear people because greater is He that is in you than he that is in this world." That Sunday I left the church filled with faith and peace that surpassed all understanding, but few days later a flashback came and left me feeling worried about the "price." I asked myself, "Didn't Jesus pay the price when he said, 'it is finished?'" I soon realized that the devil was trying to scare me with a lot of negativity. Without wasting a second, I affirmed my faith,

"Lord let your will be done in my life."

Suddenly, I felt a cool breeze around me, and a still small voice says, "I died for you, and you must witness and tell others about salvation which is a free gift of finished work." I smiled and responded aloud, "Yes Lord! The voice came to me again saying, "I shall be with you until the end." After this conversation, I realized that I had just had an encounter with the Lord without any protocol of entering in His presence. I enjoyed this fellowship even though I did not understand all the intricacies of the spiritual world. At times we do not have to follow the debunked dangerous and limiting teachings that are creeping into the church. We have to allow the Holy Spirit to teach us truth.

Though I always knew at a younger age through prophetic dreams and visions that God had chosen me for a specific mission, like what I said at the beginning of my chapter, that lack of knowledge and understanding destroyed many people including me. I was a dreamer, and all my dreams were always on point. There was no point for an interpreter - they would come to pass in seasons and people I shared with could remember. I used to prophesy unknowingly, then later someone would remind me about the prophecy. "Faith, that day you spoke about it and it has happened! Are you a prophet? "

Over time, I began to be more aware of His presence in my life. For such a long time such things were always happening but at times I did not notice that it was the Holy Spirit at work. Due to ignorance, I never fully developed my gift or put it to work. Since I was born and raised in a traditional church I had to deprogram my mind because I believed that it was only the duty of the Priest to pray and bless people. After my Pastor told me about the mantle, I was tempted to go directly after a mantle, but the Holy Spirit stopped me and recommended me to pray and fast until the mantle had been fully established. As you all know, waiting can be so hard but I grounded myself in the scriptures during that period, a lot of counselling and teachings from godly man and women. The church sent me to a Missionary school where I could simply enjoy ministry as the Lord lead.

The Holy Spirit revealed to me whatever I needed to know through dreams and visions, and more healing and deliverance sessions. Though most of my days I was lonely, left out and misunderstood (by many including my own family), I was also frustrated, felt rejected and unworthy, too. Unfortunately, you cannot write a cheque for love. I was compromising my call and trying to rebuild my friendship with others, but it was all in vain - I was simply chasing rabbits! I learned that the only thing one could do was pursuing their calling, not people. I realized that God had set me apart for His glory and He wanted me to be exceptional.

One misty day during lunch with a friend, we were discussing salvation and I asked her if she was saved because I had a vision for her. I shared it and she looked at me surprisingly and began to confess everything. She then begged me not to tell anyone that she was visiting a spirit medium for life solutions and from that day that was the end of our friendship. She could not meet eye to eye. At first I thought, "What went wrong? Have I hurt her?". When I slowly began to discover that many people were not comfortable around me and would change their directions as soon as they saw me I was convinced that darkness and light will never have a partnership. My circle got smaller and I had enough time in the secluded place to fellowship with the Lord. I learned how to surrender to His will and allow God to uproot me from my comfort zone. He put me on my mantle, like Elijah, and I began to witness some impressive natural phenomena of His presence.

Consequently, you never know what life will bring your way - God made me a woman of faith, fearless and kingdom minded. I knew nothing was impossible with God. I had so much power and spiritual authority because of the Holy Spirit which was within me. The more I encountered the Holy Spirit the more healing and deliverance God did through me. Some people confirmed that they had several dreams seeing me praying for them, they would wake up healed and began to refer others to me. God's mantle allowed me to minister in the supernatural glory. I remember I was praying for an Indian lady who wanted to commit suicide. As I was praying for her about two meters apart, she begun to manifest into a marine spirit. I heard the audible voice of God saying to me,

"Open your eyes and cast out that spirit."

When I opened my eyes, I was so scared to see how this woman was moving, then I heard again, "Don't be afraid! I am with you!", so I gained confidence and casted out the demon. She fell down and fell into a deep sleep. I thought to myself," Oh my God! What if she is dead?" then I heard again, "Fear not, I am with you." Since that day I gained so much confidence to prophecy and deliver people from demonic strongholds. The truth is, even if you have been saved or give your life to the Lord for many years it does not mean that you know everything about God's ways. My inability to clearly communicate the things that God was revealing to me through dreams and visions led me to frustration when I discovered that some Christians in my church were looking down upon me questioning my ministry. A lot of rumours, and false accusation and information was published, words were twisted and news that I was giving dreams and prophecies by dead people including my parents devastated me; that led me to a very dark place. Such trying circumstances pressed me beyond measure and I became discouraged and despondent.

Sometimes when we are faced with so much despair around us, we are left with no choice but abruptly separate ourselves from others. I thank God for the man in my life Michael, who comforted me with this word during my lows and doubting moments,

"Well, there is absolutely nothing you can do to stop people from talking about you. People will always talk about you no matter how nice or nasty you are. They even talked about Jesus, and questioned His authority so get on with your life and do what you have been call to do because one day you will be accountable in heaven alone."

Thinking of his words made me realise that sometimes the purpose is painful and hard; some people are simply jealous of your mantle. The only solution was to die to self and walk confidently in with Christ - in that case, no one will harm me with what they say about me or what they think of me. I never asked for this mantle, but grace qualifies me. I began to operate from the heart of God to bring better understanding and educating others with truth. In this process, I got a revelation that a mantle was to increase the weight of His glory in our lives so that we can be more effective in our specific assignment. We must encourage, lead with love and stand for humanity. Isolating yourself and carrying a mantle is meaningless without people to share it with. God placed it on you because He knew your heart for people.

He knew all the trials, opposition, and afflictions that I was facing was part of the package, not to hurt me or harm me but to mould me into a God-fearing woman with great wisdom and knowledge. Every challenge made me understand and embrace the reality that it is through trials that God purifies us (James 1:2-3). The more I cling to Jesus and participate in His work of restoring lives, the greater the trials and temptations I face spiritually and physically. It is true that in this life there is no sweet without sweat, there is no gain without pain and there is no test without a testimony! The enemy can accuse you and be jealous of you, but God is always faithful.

The story of Joseph has much weight and resonates in my life - I can relate to everyday. Joseph was likeable, suffered intense trials and tribulations, and was betrayed and rejected by his own people but these challenges were preparing him for his destiny. He was destined for greatness! My life was so colourful like Joseph's rainbow coat. I had different facets to my character. Whenever I think of my life, it is so incredible. Filled with the greatest levels of pain and turmoil, rejection, and judgment, it is also encompassed with a tremendous abundance of joy, prosperity, favour and blessings just like Joseph. Like the idiom, everything happens for a reason. I believe everything I faced did not stop my destiny but instead propelled me towards it. After all the emotional and draining life, today I fully operates in my spiritual mantle which I never asked for, though this ministry costs and demands a lot of responsibilities and obedience as a prerequisite. The healing and deliverance mantle is not for faint- hearted or the immature, but never be afraid to raise up when God releases such mantles over you. He will give you the supernatural ability to complete your mission and to find purpose in what you do. We all have something unique that we all never asked for and that is the mantle which gives you a sense of belonging, compassion, love, peace, courage and resilience to walk through a specific ministry or roles more anointed than others. May we all finish our race well.

Never be lacking in zeal but, keep your spiritual fervour, serving the Lord.

Romans 12:11

Million Dollar Flaws

By Dominique Cunningham - Robinson

Me: God, I don't know about this. Can you just shoot me an idea of how I can get out of this?

Him: You've got this. All you have to do is be willing to speak and I will do the rest.

Me: God are you SURE?

Him: Absolutely!

The minutes were counting down to one of the biggest moments of my life, as I prepared to stand before God and man to accept my call to preach the gospel. I sat, contemplating, and looking for the perfect reason to get out of it, but the call became stronger and stronger by the moment. The tears had a mind of their own and completely disregarded the makeup that had just been applied to my face. This indeed was a day full of being ready and unsure all at the same time. I invested weeks for this, reading, researching and writing, but no amount of preparation could prepare me for the mantle that I was on the verge of saying yes to — one that I had no way to trace. I approached my mother's house bracing myself for the response. Their excitement was overwhelming, and though I was grateful for their support, nervousness did not fail to make its presence known. As I walked in the door, tears filled my mother's eyes. My grandmother was unable to attend but insisted that I record it. There was so much happening that I could not keep up with the moment - it was all I could do to hold my composure. What I was about to say flooded my mind in the midst of all of the tears and all of the requests and as ill-equipped as I felt, I knew God had me.

I often say that God has a way that is mighty sweet and trust me this day was no different. Amidst all of the excitement and preparation to leave for the church, the twelve-year-old version of me became clear in my mind. You see, this call that I was preparing to embrace was not new news, but instead the reality of what I had tucked away in my memory bank and truthfully, I was perfectly fine with leaving it there. I was around twelve years old the first time that the reality of my destiny was revealed to me. I was introduced to church by one of my friends named Renee' who encouraged me to visit one with her; we stayed in the same apartment complex and always played together afterschool. There was a church van that came into our neighborhood weekly, so being able to catch a ride was no problem at all. My mother was apprehensive, but my desire trumped her concern. Eventually, she allowed me to go but not before she visited the church with me, so she came a few times and my sister even came along as well.

This church welcomed me with open arms and encouraged me to serve to my heart's content. I was active within the youth ministry, youth choir and even began to serve with my First Lady at the time. It was during this time that servanthood was birthed in me as they invited me to join them for times of evangelism and service in the community. While my sisters' punishment was concentrated on taking toys, games and free time away, when I got in trouble my punishment was not being able to participate in activities within the ministry. One day we were in service in a room fully charged with the presence of God. As songs of praise and worship were going forth, the prophetic Word began to flow. There was a woman there who was going forth with the rest of us; all of a sudden, she turned and pointed to me. In that moment I looked behind me thinking,

"She could not possibly be talking to me!"

71

With big, disbelieving eyes, I pointed to myself only to receive her reply, "Yes you! I am talking to you! There is an anointing on your life that will cause you to make a difference in your generation. So many will come if you simply say YES! Even older women will be changed and listen to the words that come out of your mouth!" After delivering these words to me, she began to speak in tongues for a short while.

For the next six years, the seed of servanthood continued to be watered and nurtured within me; it is a seed that I will be forever grateful for. To my Pastor at the time, I was often referred to as "his cheerleader." I was always excited about the Word of God and anticipating the next move of God! We often traveled out of the area to fellowship with other churches and I was responsible for making sure that everyone was present and accounted for along with other tasks and responsibilities. Though it had not been said, I knew that I had been set apart as a model teenager within ministry, but the day came when our relationship changed.

When charged with such a task to serve and lead, whether said or not said, disappointment hits differently. For years, things had been going well, but at the age of eighteen things shifted upon the news of me being pregnant with my daughter. To me, it was a weight that I never expected, being that I knew others who were doing the same thing but got different responses and whose actions remained hidden. Here I was in this moment, disappointed in myself and wondering if I would be able to ever recover from this place.

Despite the situation I found myself in, God's Word came as an echo more clearly than ever. Every part of me for a time wished that the Word spoken over me had never been said, especially out loud. I was so startled by the Word given that I did not even have the audacity to tell her "no" or "that Word isn't for me!" Even at twelve years old, it was as if I would not be able to deny it even if I wanted to. Then the thought hit me - if she HAD to say it, why did it have to be in the presence of so many people who would later have to witness me go through this place of perceived failure? Can you imagine sitting on the brink of a life-changing moment that, to the world, disqualifies you only to find that God is using it to QUALIFY you? I could not make sense of it, but at the same time I knew that it was something I eventually had to accept.   The echoes of "expectation" were hard to ignore, as I went from simply being Dominique to being, "the girl that got called out that day in church." I spent days and months waiting for God to change His mind – after all, I was now involved in "visible sin." Even after having my daughter, I had to adopt a "poker face." I was not sure how I would ever be able to live up to the words sent by God and delivered by that woman six years before; my heart questioned the ability, but my spirit remained ready.

As time progressed, the mantle on my life became even the more sure. Though the whole world was not present in my church that day, it sure did feel as if they were. Every time something happened, it seemed as if everyone always came to me, asking for prayer and wisdom. Prayer requests seemed to come with the opening statement,

"If God doesn't hear anyone else's prayers, we know He hears yours!"

No matter how much I tried to recommend others for the task, it seemed as if I was always the chosen one. As God always seemed to do, as soon as I would accept the request and open my mouth, His Word flowed through me like water, leaving everyone including me surprised at the end. What always blessed my soul was God's response, as testimonies of answered prayers flooded my ears. All I could do was give God praise over and over again for being willing to hear me and even more willing to respond.

As the day of my initial sermon approached, I knew that I would eventually have to share the news. Hesitant but willing, I finally shared with my family and friends only to find that many were not surprised but instead, waiting for the day that I would finally share what had been hovering over my life for so long. The days leading up to my public declaration seemed to go so slow yet so fast all at the same time. I will never forget receiving my clergy shirt and finally coming to a place of receiving where God was leading me into. There are not many moments that compare to the great reveal, when you look in the mirror and see yourself in that shirt knowing that life as you know it is truly about to change.

Despite my inner battle to find a way out of the call, God gave me one Word of encouragement,

Obedience is so much better.

Before going forth to minister, my Pastors gave me the charge, to preach the Word of God with power and to make it my business not to cry before releasing what had been entrusted in me to share. This day was not the first day I had approached the podium, as I had led prayer in that same place Sunday after Sunday, nevertheless this time was different. As the microphone was passed over to me, it was as if for a moment it had become a baton. It did not matter that I had been a single mother, the mantle was greater. The fact of how many times I felt like a failure did not count against me, because the mantle was greater. There was no disqualification, though I could not trace this call to any of my relatives, that could take me out of the race, all that mattered was that I gave God a YES and that He accepted it. That day, I finally saw what that lady saw in church years before, a vessel for God that would be willing to stand before man and declare His Word with boldness and no shame.

At the conclusion, my Pastors presented me with my minister's license but not before anointing me. With one in

74

front of me and one behind, they anointed me in front of our church, my family and friends and poured from a place that I had never experienced; just as I could not deny the impartation at twelve years old, I could not deny it in this moment either. Prior to that day, I had operated in ministry to the capacity of a lay member - the youth ministry, evangelism, and prayer, but on that day, I realized that life as I knew it would never be the same as my YES crushed every generational curse and released blessings upon blessings for my family. It was then that I realized that God just needed one to accept the call for the sake of the bloodline, and the someone He chose was me. From that day to this I still stand, amazed and in awe of who He is and how He saw so much in me, despite my unbelief that He had the ability to bring it out. I remain grateful that He never took my doubt into consideration, but instead considered the mantle on my life to be greater.

**"Before I formed you in the womb I knew you [and approved of you as My chosen instrument],
And before you were born I consecrated you [to Myself as My own];
I have appointed you as a prophet to the nations."**

-Jeremiah 1:5

"Passion Fueling Purpose"

By Zulema Nicole Powell-Settle

This is dedicated to all the men, women and adolescents who cannot understand the adversity that they are going through or have experienced. Understand that being in a mantle that you did not ask for is all part of His plan and the blueprint in which He created within you for the greater of good. Remember pressure creates diamonds and in God's eye you are His diamond; He will not put you under something you cannot endure or something that you cannot not handle and arise from.

Trust and stand on His Word, for I know what my Father can do. I am a witness to Gods unchanging hands and what He can do when purpose has been activated down on the inside and you are able to be fruitful and multiply the goodness of what was planted.

I would like to thank God for never taking His hands off me and keeping me kept even when I was not clear on things. When you are covered by God's armor there is nothing that the blood cannot and would not cover. Glory be to God! When you allow God to renew and restore you for the purpose in what he has created, it does not matter where you come from, but all that matters is where you are going!

Your passion is your "what" - what you feel, what comes easy and what gives you the energy. Your purpose is your "why", the reason for your existence. Come on walk with me let me explain how my God laid the pieces and how one can go through the fire and come out not burned or singed. There is more to you then what you think; there is so much more beyond everything that you can ever imagine lying deep on the inside of you. My purpose is to restore, renew, empower and serve however my Father sees fit. My vision is to support, inspire and educate people to achieve the lifestyle they want and desire, with a full understanding and implementation of how my Father has been calling me.

Growth is painful! Change is painful, however you cannot have change without challenge in order to acquire what God has for you. I am convinced that the hardest language to speak for some is the "Truth." I know for me to follow the path that was set for me I must listen to God's Words as He speaks to me; when I do it becomes a lot easier for me to produce the truth. A year ago, I would have never pictured my life the way it is now. Just two years prior I was homeless, sleeping in my car, and everything was falling quicker than the beats of a heart. Often people that criticize your life are usually the same people that do not know the price you paid to get where you are today. When I look back on the past, I smile and say to myself "I never thought I could do it, but I did." I overcame all the different adversity that came in my life to bring me down and meant for me to fail. You cannot control how others perceive you or what they think of you, no matter how hard you try. That is why it is so important to live authentically according to the principles God has written on your heart. Practice those principles today and every day, without attachment to a specific result. Just do your best without judging yourself.

I was standing on a line between giving up and seeing how much more she can take. When He made the woman, He did not just decorate the outside, but He decorated the inside of the woman, too; He also placed beauty in Spirit. God will speak to your heart "Well Done." There is always a process that leads to promise. You can never receive a blessing and think you cannot circumvent the pain.

Have you ever just felt like you heard a voice say, "Move now! Just go!", but you sit there not able to do anything but wonder if that message was God's impartation to you or simply, you talking to yourself? Think about how often we hear that sound saying "go" and we stand in complete confusion not sure what to do. You ask loudly, "God send me a sign so I know it is you!" Even the stronger of us need to be refilled and restored. We tend to pour so much into others but find ourselves looking around for someone to pour back out into us and sometimes it is in the worst way, a complete 9-1-1 moment.

For I consider [from the standpoint of faith] that the sufferings of the present life are not worthy to be compared with the glory that is about to be revealed to us *and* in us!

Romans 8:18

Let me just be transparent - of what I have known for the greater part of my life, however, I was running from it. Maybe because I did not feel worthy, that I could measure up or that I was not enough. These doubts began to deplete my faith; I found myself saying:

"Oh, you are just tripping."

"You do not hear anyone talking to you in your ear."

"Clearly that is not God because you are just doing too much."

I had to completely talked myself out of the feelings and what I was hearing simply because I knew that did not sound like my Daddy's voice! Despite my position, I would have dreams and see them come to pass; I would see a whole situation and then see it happen in real life. Even to this day, I can be around people and completely speak up on what is going on with them or feel someone else's pain! A I was aware of this but would just pass it off as a coincidence. I would soon come to realize none of it was coincidence. Again, I hear a voice say, "Nothing I do is

79

coincidence. My response showed up quickly in the form of "huh, what!" Then I would always begin looking around like I was confused and puzzled.

This is all fact, never judge a book by the cover! You will never know what lies between the other pages if you stay stuck on the cover. This is your time, this your moment. God is preparing you right now because He is about to release a special grace to help you accomplish your dream.

Surrender! Do not ignore the call; I promise you this, you will get tired of running before He ever stops chasing you down. It is important to understand that it is not how people view you but how God views you and what you believe in what he views. It is not what I have been through that defines me - it is how I have gotten through it and what I am because of it. My father clears all paths. Face Fears with Faith and everything will turn out fine.

"My maker is my mirror"

Lord pull me, push me, whatever you have to just keep me. The power through the process is real and the unimaginable things that one goes through and still continues to smile is indescribable. It is by the grace and mercy of God that I have not lost my mind. It is the favor that is over my life, it is the blood that covers me.

Father I am still thanking you through is all. I am exactly where I am meant to be. I do not know what is next however I trust in God and know that everything is exactly the way it is supposed to be. I have decided to Leave it in the hands of my Father, for the battle is not mine it is the Lord's. I now understand that when God chose you there was a purpose, not just a want. There is a difference in being called and being appointed. When you are called, He is preparing you to be appointed to what He has for you. Being called does not mean you have arrived. It does not mean there will be no adversity, being called does not mean everything will come easy.

When my Father speaks to me, He says:

"My child, now that I have your full attention, I need you to know that being "called" means, I am preparing and grooming you for your next and preparing you for what you asked for getting you ready. Understand my child that sometimes it will not be just what you asked for, it will also be what you need and did not know that you lacked. People have been trying to put you where you do not belong. You cannot fit or place a square inside of a circle - it does not belong and will never fit."

I now understand on a different level that my God has been calling me. I realize that yes, there is a reason for going through all that I have endured. God has me in the process so that the purpose can be birthed. My father God in heaven knows that when He created me, He placed some gifts deep inside that is the perfect image of Him and who He is.

Even now, He says:

I am going to use you through visions and the prophetic. The prophecy is in your voice - you have what it takes. It is not about what you look like or how you fit in with the missionaries. It is about being able to give the word, preach the word and break it down so others will understand. I need for you to deliver it how I bring it to you.

Understand, what HE (GOD) gives you! The moment you are ready to quit is usually the moment right before the miracle happens. Do not give up now, you are closer to your miracle than you can see. There are times you will be given intuition, or should I say discernment; you will just know something and will not be able to explain it. You may not have facts to back it up, but you just know. Do not overlook it or talk yourself out of it, because that is God giving you inside information. Trust it and trust Him for He will never steer His child wrong. Just as child must pass through a tiny channel on it is a way from womb into life, is just the same with us. We must go through things in order to get where we are supposed to be. I can truly say that I am loving my road that I have traveled because the best is yet to come. The bad has made me stronger, the tears have cleaned my soul my niece and my boys keep me going!

Thank you, God for who I am at the end of the day. I can never thank You enough!

"The Mystery Behind My Mantle"

By Janelle Strickland

I had just finished preaching and there had been a great move of God. I was sitting reflective of all that God had done and I began to have a conversation with him.

"God, this is not fair. Where did all of this come from? I don't have a clue why you gave all of this to me. I'm not even confident in how any of this works. I wish my grandpa Strickland was still here. He would know exactly how to explain all of this to me. The reality is he transitioned from this life a long time ago and he left me to carry on what his father gave him, and what he gave my father and now what has passed to me, the mantle I never asked for."

I gave my life to the Lord and got saved initially when I was a youth. Like many others before me I felt a tug at my heart after a message preached by my godfather. I came to the altar, recited the sinner's prayer and got saved. No one ever talked to me about being saved or how to live right. There was no celebration or conversations about what had just taken place. My life continued as it always had. In my heart something different took place but no one took out time to even teach me about what had happened. After that, I gave it a little thought but with no one to turn to about it, life went on just as it always had and things began to get worse. I did not think God even cared about me. That moment I went to the altar and gave God my heart became a very distant memory.

Things became so bad that I attempted suicide. I ran away from home and was living on my own, was taking care of myself at the age of fourteen and was forced to go and live with my father and his abusive wife; eventually I went to stay with my grandparents most of the time. Granddaddy was a Pastor, Elder and held positions within the United Holy Church of America. He helped many up-and-coming ministers as they matured in their calling and developed them for kingdom purpose. I only wish that I had that same experience with him.

One day I was outside playing and roller skating on the concrete patio but stopped because I heard something. I left the patio and stood on the grass and looked up. I do not know how long I had been standing there when I realized Granddaddy was beside me. He asked me what I was looking at? I responded with a question of my own. I asked him,

"Don't you hear it?"

"Hear what?" he replied. I explained that I could hear voices and singing coming out of the sky. I assumed that he could hear it too. He asked me what the voices were saying and what the singing sounded like. I tried my best to explain it to him. He patiently listened to my childish descriptions of what was singing and scriptures. I was literally hearing the word of God coming out of heaven, through the clouds. It sounded so beautiful. I have never heard such beautiful sounds here on earth ever again. My granddaddy patiently stood with me as I told him what I heard. He did not say much. He watched me and listened to what I had to share. This was only the beginning of a journey to discovering the many gifts, callings, assignments and mantles that were in my life. I did not realize then, what I was embarking on. I now wonder what my granddaddy thought after that experience.

Living with my grandparents was the best part of my life. It was there that I felt, knew and experienced real love. They lived out what was preached and taught. I saw the evidence of the Word of God in their daily lives. While living there I would experience really bad nose bleeds. I would wake up my grandparents and my grandma would get towels and cold compresses. She would tell granddaddy to get the Bible. Granddaddy would go to Ezekiel 16:6 and read it and pray for me. Granny would hold me close to her with the towel to my face and pray as well. Just like it started it stopped. Multiple times, this would happen, and their response would always be the same - the word of God and prayer. Little did I know that these events were shaping my spiritual walk and preparing me for where God was calling me to.

Every Sunday my grandma and I would get ready for church while my granddaddy would go to the hospital and visit the sick before we headed to his church in Durham, North Carolina. It was not uncommon that he would engage me as a part of his preparation for the sermon he was preaching that day. He would ask me to read text from the Bible or an excerpt from a book while he was driving to church. At home I watched him as he would retreat to his study. When he closed the door, we were all instructed to keep quiet and never to disturb him. He would go in and stay for hours. Sometimes, I would hear him praying. I did not realize then that this was a very sacred time before the Lord and that he was shut in to hear from Him what to share with the people he pastored as well as the many others who called on him and pulled on him for counseling, prayer, and guidance. Watching him serve the people of God and fill his assignment in the kingdom of God selflessly became the memories that I would tug on for clarity of what God was calling me to.

Before me there was another one who the mantle was passed to, my father. Early on in his life my granddaddy prayed for him and he miraculously recovered. Suffering from Cushing's disease, losing his adrenal glands and almost losing his life, he too answered the call to ministry. When my granddaddy was very ill and bedridden, God used my father to pray for him and God raised him up. Miracles had happened long before this and those moments shaped the faith that my granddaddy and father had. I never met my great grandfather, but the stories I have heard about him were the evidence that there was a generational link to the gifts I possess, and the mantles I would carry. No one took time to explain, what that would be like or what to expect. Hearsay and the occasional stories shared by family members is all that I got besides what I saw in my grandparents' life from living with them and going to church with them for years.

As the years passed, even more unexplainable things began to happen to me. I had many deja vu experiences. I would see things on the news or hear people talking about things that happened and I had already seen it, dreamed it or it was as if I had already experienced it. When I shared it with certain people, they accused me of dealing with witchcraft or having ESP. I had no idea what either of those things were as a young teen. I stopped sharing what I saw. I felt the negativity and the sting of being considered different and strange; as a result, I was labeled. It was said that these strange occurrences were the result of my mother's drug use, my being exposed to the smoke or that I was using drugs like her none of which was true. I could not explain that what I was watching as I had already seen and felt before. All I could say was that I had already experienced it. I could only remember the previous experiences after they actually occurred. Ignorantly, I began to explain these unusual occurrences as some sort of psychic or mystical power. I began to do my own investigation through books in my school library. These resource materials almost led me to a pathway to certain darkness.

Although I was not close to God, I felt I was okay and that I could wait until I got old and then I would do the things old people do, go to church and their whole life at that point would evolve around what they did for the Lord. That was because at that age they could not do anything else. They were old. Me being young and quite spiritually unaware of what my future would hold, I lived my life my way. I would often ask aimlessly to whatever force had given me this gift of experiencing the future before it happened, to let me remember these occurrences when I experienced them. This would give me an upper hand. For years the memory of these occurrences were only sparked when the event actually happened. I almost became numb to it. I would simply see something I had previously experienced and react as if it were nothing because, I had already experienced it; this was not a surprise. This was connected to many spiritual gifts that were a result of the mantles, I never asked for.

WHAT IS A MANTLE?

A mantle is a predetermined, scriptural metaphor, symbolic for a calling, ministry, anointing, assignment, gift or even a given position or office given to an individual by God.

I derived this definition of what a mantle is after reading several different definitions and reading multiple resources about spiritual mantles. Based on my understanding and experiences, a mantle can come through both a natural blood line as well as a spiritual transfer by one whom you have served as in the biblical example of Elijah and Elisha. The cloak that the prophet Elijah wore fell to Elisha as a material evidence of the divine transfer of the mantle he left in the earth for Elisha to now receive and carry. Many see it as a simple piece of clothing. It was so much more as a personal in-depth study will reveal. Little did I know that three generations on the Strickland side would create the mantles that I would have to carry and live out. In addition to that I was also told by my mother that her grandfather, George Newby also was a believer in God and lived a very strict godly lifestyle as a result of his relationship with the Lord. Now here I am, a teenager, having supernatural experiences in the spirit realm on a regular basis all because of the mantles, my former family members left in the earth. I had no idea how to even begin to process any of this. I never chose the mantles. The mantles chose me!

Life went on and I got married and had children of my own; I had given my life to the Lord and did my best to live a godly life. In my late twenties, God showed up and called me into the ministry. By this time, I was having dreams of the future, seeing visions of things past, present and future and warring against demons in my sleep, so much so, my husband thought I was possessed. He could not understand the incidents of warfare in my sleep that resulted in physical bruises on my body. He thought I was hurting myself on purpose because I needed a demonic entity cast out of me. As I began to preach and teach, God was using me in ways I never imagined. I was preaching at huge conferences, praying for long lines of people and seeing God move. While all of this was amazing, I still had no real idea of what a mantle was and how it applied to me.

AND THEN... LIFE HAPPENED.

Life took a drastic terrible turn. Divorce and a terrible custody battle left me weary, broken and I walked away from the Lord, the church and ministry. I was turned on by those I had prayed for, stood in the gap with and God used me to minister to. The church and all who were a part of the fellowship I belonged to, cast me as many things I was not. I tried my best to run away from them and the pain they caused as well as the God I blamed for everything that happened. All I did was run in a big 'ole circle right back to the place I started at, God.

After all of that, I went back to the God that I saw my granddaddy and grandma serve and live for in front of me for so many years. I went to the God I has seen answer their prayers and stop the nose bleeds, heal the sick and work in their lives. I went to the God granddaddy had preached about. I went to the God who saved me at a young age at the altar where I first accepted him as lord and Savior of my life. I went to the God that granddaddy said loved me no matter what. It was here that I gave my life back to the Lord and started over. I felt that I had strayed so far that I was starting over from the point of initial grace and salvation of that little girl who went to the altar alone, said the sinner's prayer and accepted Jesus as her personal Savior. I did not realize that the mantles never left and that I was selected by God for the mantles that were transferred to me. Feeling totally disqualified of ever be used by God anywhere near where I was before, I backslide after the divorce; I was simply okay with just being saved and filled with the Holy Ghost. I actually told God I had no desire to be in the pulpit or ministry ever again. I discounted the mantles because people disqualified me, and I felt it was only natural for me to feel the same way and disqualify myself.

I felt I was blessed just to be saved and that things would never go back to what they were when I was in ministry before. I felt that I had disappointed my grandparents and so many others in the twenty years I was not active in ministry. During that twenty years, I was under another mantle I did not ask for, a divorced, fallen minister. This was the mantle my father left me. Many assumed that I would end up staying in this place. Not accepting that as my end, I executed the plan God had for my redemption. From that moment, I took the steps I had not seen my father take. Although he had decided his place was to leave ministry and not go back, I refused to follow suit. Along with the fall was an option of forgiveness and grace - both of us had an option. We chose differently.

Once again, God disturbed me about ministry. I told the Lord, I did not want any part of being a minister and if I was ever to go into a pulpit again, He would have to do it with no help from me. I tried to ignore it but got to the point that I could not even sleep. God would not leave me alone. Finally, out of sheer exhaustion, I went to my Pastors and told them what God had been dealing with me concerning ministry. Pastor Omar said that he knew it and that he wanted to say something, but God would not allow it. I explained to him why God would not allow that. God had to do it! On Sunday August 21, 2016 I was licensed again as a minister and then February 18, 2018 I was ordained an Elder. I was good. This was a huge victory! I could see myself serving in this place until......

I found myself experiencing more of what occurred in my youth - supernatural spiritual experiences. I no longer had to pray to remember what I dreamed, and my visions were clear. I began to see the past, present, future, demons and angels, and experienced being able to hear and see in the spirit what was going on. I began to see the death angel and who he was coming for. I began to see what was coming for geographical areas, illnesses in people's bodies and when attacks came, their places of origin. I could look at a person and see things about them and they did not even have to tell me. I kept a respectful distance from people because I did not need nor want them to share what was going on with them. I have the real Holy Ghost and anything that I need to know, God will show me. Without knowing, God would minister through me and the recipient would know that it was God and not me. As time progressed, I was being used to heal others, miracles, signs and wonders were coming forth through me and I had no idea where all this was coming from. So here I am, operating in the prophetic, seeing visions and dreams, having visitations of angels, cherubim and even heavenly experiences where I have even seen the gates of the entrance to heaven and smelled the scent of hell and heard the sounds of torment of those who have their place there. I can see the visible presence of God, the shekinah glory. With all of this, you would think that it is an amazing and awesome experience to carry these gifts that are associated with the mantles that have come through three prior generations and from being a servant to previous and my current leaders who also carry several mantles themselves. They were the first people who were able to demonstrate what I was experiencing and explain some of what I was carrying.

The mantles I carry are from people in my blood line that I never met or even had conversations with. There are other mantles that I carry that came from my leaders. For years I felt different and no one would even acknowledge what I was carrying or even help to mature it. After being used of God, I often felt confused as to where all of this was coming from, but then I began to seek out what mantles I had and their source. Some mantles I could trace back to a source, but the source was no longer in the earth.

In all of this I have learned this truth,

Those who did not choose you cannot disqualify you from the mantle God preassigned to you. You cannot even disqualify yourself.

The Living Mantle

By LaTasha W. Tisdale

On September 19, 2017, a demon-fighting, Bible-reading, God-fearing, Jesus-chasing, glory-giving, hell-shaking, faith-having, Word-believing Intercessor and Evangelist was called to her heavenly home. This beautiful soul's name is Ada A. Watson. Mother Ada (as she was known in the Church) loved the Lord with every fiber of her being. The day she gave God her YES, she never looked back. Now, with her YES, she endured so many things, both naturally and spiritually. Her toughest battle was her fight with stroke. On a sunny day in 2007, Mother Ada suffered a stroke right in her lovely home. During her rehabilitation period, Mother Ada got upset with God and even stopped praying and praising God. The thought of Him made her question His decision, His purpose in her life and the YES she gave Him! Mother Ada began to question,

"Why would God, the One who loved me so much, the One who told me that I was the apple of His eye, the One who would move mountains for me, allow something like this to happen to me?"

God answered her question with a quite simple reply,

"Why not you? You told Me that you will live and die for Me. You said that I can use you any way that I pleased. So why not you?"

This made Mother Ada repent quickly and return to her post of prayer and praise, even from her bed and wheelchair. So, we fast forward two years later, and Mother Ada suffered another stroke; this time she becomes bed ridden. Did she get upset? Nope! Did she question God again? Not at all! What did she do you ask? She praised God like never before. She ministered to her husband and to her children. She shared the gospel to the nurses, doctors, and rehabilitation specialists. She kept a smile on her face and a song on her lips. Mother Ada did all these things and more until her final breath.

One year later...

On September 19, 2018, a sweet, God-fearing, Jesus-chasing, Word-believing, Bible-reading Choir member and Sunday school teacher walked into her bedroom. As she began to pass by her desk chair, a heavy weight fell upon her shoulders. This was not the kind of weight that you feel when your life is turned upside or when everyone dumps their burdens on your shoulders – this weight was different. This weight had power. This weight had authority. This weight was the kind that makes the very gates of hell tremble. To give a visual illustration of this weight, it was not like the yolk that an ox wears around its neck, but instead like a weighted blanket; and on this day God oh-so gracefully draped it over the shoulders of LaTasha Watson Tisdale.

Tasha, as she is known by everyone, immediately knew what just taken place, "The Mantle Shift", the changing of the guards and it happened without skipping a beat or missing a step. It was seamless and well planned, however, in Tasha's case, it was totally unexpected. In her spirit, Tasha immediately began asking God why. Her mind began to flood with all the reasons why she was the wrong candidate for the Call. The doubts, the insecurities, and the fears began whirling around like a fierce wind. Tasha tried to shake the feeling, but it would not go away. For months, Tasha toiled in her spirit about what God had revealed to her. Part of her wanted to share the news with her husband, but she was unsure about what to say or how to say it. Tasha even wanted to share the news with her spiritual leaders, but that deemed to be a major issue.

See, her spiritual leaders had a philosophy about "women in ministry." According to their understanding of **2 Timothy 2:12** (*I do not permit a woman to teach or to exercise authority over a man; she is to remain quiet: Berean Study Bible*), they believed that it was wrong for women to preach. Now, they were okay with them doing "women-appropriate" things in ministry such as teaching Children's Sunday School, leading the Hospitality Ministry, being a Choir Director, leading the Women's Ministry, or being a part of the Intercession Ministry, but that is where it stopped. Of course, this caused a major anxiety in Tasha's heart, mind, and spirit. Daily she fought with the desire to please God and answer the Call; or to just leave it alone and continue to serve God in the position she currently was in.

April 2019 (Messenger Conversation) ...

One late night while Tasha was babysitting, God finally convinced Tasha to open about her internal struggles:

TT: *So, I have been toiling with something in my spirit for a little while. I have been trying to talk about it, but the subject tends to get changed. It became more prevalent after your Live Pastor @Brandi L Rojas about "Mantles" and them being passed down from generation to generation. So, on my late Mother's side, her grandfather was a pastor. After he passed there was no one else to take upon the mantle, therefore, it fell upon my mother and she was called to be an Evangelist. Since my mother passed, there is NO ONE else in my family as for it to fall upon, well at least that is what I thought.*

PBR: *My only question - who gave God a YES???*

TT: *ME!*

January 2020...

Tasha's toil continued into late December 2019. Even after much council from her Pastor friend, Pastor Brandi Rojas, she still could not build the courage to say something to her spiritual leaders. When Tasha finally shared the news with her husband, Darryl, he did what he does best - ENCOURAGE!! Darryl reminded Tasha of her vow to God: **To serve Him with all her heart, mind, body, and soul; and no matter how much she tried, she could not run away from the Call.**

As Tasha listened intently, her spirit and God began to finally agree, until that dreadful day in late January. After a soul-stirring 21-day fast, Tasha and her husband made a major life changing decision - to leave the church they had been members of for over ten years and join a new one! As liberated as they two of them felt about their decision, there were others who were not! As a result, their former spiritual leaders called a meeting to discuss the SUDDEN departure. Despite the wisdom shared regarding the pending meeting, and feeling the need to make all things right, they made the decision to go against the Godly advice shared. They went to the meeting ready to defend their decision and to say their final goodbyes but immediately, the meeting went south.

Attack came from every angle possible. They did all they could to stand strong and firm with as much power they could muster in their responses to each and every question. As things were being revealed, the need to share the revelation received about what God had been doing in Tasha's life become the topic of discussion - the reality of the "Mantle Shift." As she spoke with confidence about what God had revealed to her months prior, her former spiritual leaders looked at one another and one even shook his head in disbelief. As she finished, her former spiritual leader looked her in the eyes and said the words she never expected he would say,

"Tasha, you know what the Word says about women preachers. I would just hate for you think that God called you to do this, then you die and go to hell."

98

Her heart immediately crushed into a thousand pieces and sank to the pit of her stomach. Once again, she questioned God about why He called her and why she had to be one?

May 2020 (Mother's Day) ...

Months had gone by and Tasha began to recover from that spiritual tragedy. She was finally under the spiritual covering that would help her grow into her Mantle - the same Mantle that she was ready to give up on. It was Mother's Day during Life Café, that Tasha shared a beautiful testimony about her mother and how this was the first year she could smile about her memory and not cry. During Praise and Worship, God began moving mightily in the room. As Tasha raised her hands in worship, she began to feel a presence that she was oh-so familiar with. As she continued to press, the presence became stronger around her, until God revealed exactly what it was - the mantle that had become realized in her life. She praised God with all of her might in that moment, feeling every impartation the Holy Spirit had placed upon her mother. God allowed Pastor Brandi to see this in the spirit, and He instructed for her to say these words:

Tasha, this may sound strange, but you no longer need to wear that white flower in memory of your mother. She is not dead she is alive! Her spirit lives on through YOU!"

TODAY...

It has been a very long and interesting journey for me. I literally went from receiving an unexpected "Mantle Shift", to it almost being ripped off me to finally realizing that it LIVES inside of me. I still have so much growing and learning to do. Yes, I know that I will have to endure many trials and that my faith will be tested time and time again. I am fully aware that there will be attacks from every given angle. However, I am ready!!! I am ready for the fight!! I am ready for the WIN!!

I am READY to WALK in my Call!!

Brandi L. Rojas

**Wife I Mother I Pastor I Author I Mentor I
Entrepreneur I Visionary Author**

Pastor Brandi L. Rojas is a native and resident of Greensboro, N.C. She serves with her Husband, Pastor Omar Rojas at Maximizing Life Family Worship Center in Greensboro, N.C., a vision God birthed through them in 2015. Rojas has been in Dance Ministry for over 20 years and is a 2009 graduate of the School of Disciples taught under the late Bishop Otis Lockett, Sr. Pastor Rojas was licensed to preach the Gospel on February 27, 2011 in Thomasville, N.C., and as a result DYmondFYre Global Ministries was born. Rojas was ordained as an Ordained Elder June 2012, was installed as Pastor with her Husband, Pastor Omar Rojas in January 2013 and now serves as Executive Pastor for the vision God has assigned to them through #MaxLife.

Since that time, she and her Husband, also known as #TeamRojas, by God's mandate, have been honored in the marketplace and birthed several evangelistic causes. In 2013, Rojas was named Sweetheart of the Triad, an award given based on community involvement. In January 2014, Rojas opened FYreDance Studios and Liturgical Arts

Consulting which provides on-site instruction, virtual teaching, consultation services, choreography services and deliverance and healing dance encounters. In that same year, after serving with Pastor Cassandra Elliott and The Gathering Experience for two years, she began serving and currently serves as the Lead Dance Vessel Coordinator for this time of worship amongst those who are hungry, thirsty and desperate for the presence of God. The following year a prayer walk initiative was created to bring the local churches and community together to work together and help lead the lost to Jesus Christ and empower the world through a vehicle called The Gatekeeper's Legacy; she has also served as part of the planning and leadership committee for the National Day of Prayer for the City of Greensboro and currently serves as the youngest committee member, only African-American and only female on the core team.

In February 2016, Rojas launched out again to begin The Legacy Ladies Fellowship, an organization created to help women of God pray, push and live the reality of what God has called them to do. Most recently to this list of mandates, The CrossOver Resource Center was added, working to provide solutions for life's transitions to the community. Rojas released her first book in June 2016 entitled In the Face of Expected Failure and her sophomore project, Humpty Dumpty in Stilettos: The Great Exchange, in

November 2016. It was with the second book release Fiery Beacon Publishing House was launched, serving current and upcoming authors, playwrights, poets, blog writers and more. Humpty Dumpty in Stilettos was nominated for the national Literary Trailblazer of the Year Award in June 2017 by the Indie Author Legacy Award in Baltimore, Maryland and in July 2017 she was noted as an International Best-Selling Author for her part in a collaborative effort called Stories from the Pink Pulpit: Women in Ministry Speak. Rojas is also a two-time nominee for Trailblazer of the Year, Choreographer of the Year and Women of Inspiration with ACHI Women Supporting Women, Inc. Since that time, Rojas has released several other literary works including, but not limited to, Rehobeth Church Road: Suicide in the Pulpit, When Legacy Arises from the Threshing Floor: A Collective of Trials and Tribulations Superseded by Undeniable Triumphs, and Before You Hit 40: 41 Pivotal Wisdom Nuggets!

In the Marketplace, Pastor Rojas is also known for her progressive efforts through her travel company, Fiery Beacon Travel and the international platform of Surge365 where she makes it a priority to share the reality and necessity of multiple streams of income which empowers the home, community, nation and world. Pastor Rojas is grateful and humbled at how God continues to expand the entire vision, not just to the United States, but internationally as well.

#Team Rojas are the proud parents of five children. Pastor Brandi Rojas is a Worshiper, Servant, Praise Vessel, and Prayer Warrior, but most of all, she is a vessel who is on fire for God.

Wife I Mother I Pastor I Author I Mentor I Entrepreneur I Visionary

Maximizing Life Family Worship Center

https://www.facebook.com/MaximizingLife/

Fiery Beacon Publishing House, LLC

(Consulting/Publishing Group)

https://www.facebook.com/FieryBeaconPHLLC/

Fiery Beacon Travel

https://www.facebook.com/thelegacybuilder/

IG and Twitter: @allthingsdymondfyre and @maxlifedfg

Fiery Beacon
PUBLISHING HOUSE

Greensboro, North Carolina

Phone: (501) 500-3973

fierybeaconcpg@gmail.com

www.ingramcontent.com/pod-product-compliance
Lightning Source LLC
Chambersburg PA
CBHW052140090426
42741CB00009B/2159